PUTTING 5S TO WORK

PUTTING 5S TO WORK

A Practical Step-by-Step Approach

By
Hiroyuki Hirano

Chairman, JIT Management Laboratory, Co.

P H P   I N S T I T U T E ,   I N C .
TOKYO • KYOTO • NEW YORK • SINGAPORE

This book was originally published in Japanese by
Nikkan Kogyo Shimbunsha under the title of *Kakaricho, hancho
no tameno 5S teichakuka wan, tsuu, surii*,
copyright © 1992 Hiroyuki Hirano.
English translation copyright
© 1993 by PHP Institute, Inc.
Translated by Birmingham Brains Trust

•

Published by PHP Institute, Inc.
Tokyo Head Office:
3-10, Sanbancho, Chiyoda-ku, Tokyo 102 Japan
Kyoto Head Office:
11 Kitanouchicho, Nishikujo, Minami-ku, Kyoto 601 Japan
Distributed in North America and Europe by
PHP Institute of America, Inc. 420 Lexington Avenue
Suite 646, New York 10170 U.S.A., and in Asia
and Oceania by PHP International (S) Pte., Ltd.,
20 Cecil Street, #15-07 The Exchange, Singapore 0104,
The Republic of Singapore; and in Japan by
PHP Institute, Inc.

•

•

Printed in Japan by Tosho Printing Co., Ltd.
Typesetting by Asahi Media International Corporation.
Cover design by Michael Gilmore and
book design and layout by Koitsu Taniguchi.
The main text is set in 10-point Times Roman Linotronic 300.

•

First Edition, March 1993
Seventh Printing, August 1995
ISBN4-569-53935-1

Contents

STEP

I

TIDY UP FIRST
(Active 5S)

PREPARATION:
RECORDING THE PRESENT SITUATION

> ■ Before launching into 5S activities, the very first thing to do is to take photographs around the workplace. These will be very useful for comparison purposes when 5S is in full swing.

Checkpoints

 1. Clearly determine the position each picture was taken from, so that you will be able to have *before* and *after* photographs.

2. Date all photos. If possible, use a camera which prints the date on the negative.

3. Take color photos. This will be useful in facilitating organization by color.

Take photos from the same position

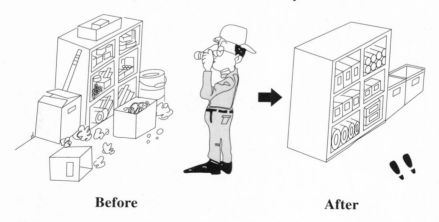

Before   **After**

PROCESS 1:
ELIMINATING UNNECESSARY ITEMS (CLEARING UP)

1-1. Can You Find Any Unnecessary Items?

- In fact, there are many unnecessary items in any factory.
- By *unnecessary*, we mean things which are not needed for present production.
- Have a good look round your own workplace.

Checkpoints: Do these situations look familiar?

 1. Raw materials: what are they used for?

2. Materials storage: when will they be used?

13

3. Parts on shelves: it's not enough just to lay them out neatly!

4. Parts on shelves: do you know what is where?

1-2. The Red Tag Tactic: Visual Clearing Up

1. What is the Red Tag Tactic?

- This is a vital clearing up technique.
- As soon as an unnecessary item is identified, it is marked with a red tag (*akafuda*) so that anybody can see clearly what needs to be eliminated or moved.
- The use of red tags can be one secret to a company's survival.

 Checkpoints: Procedures for implementing the Red Tag Tactic

1 STARTING POINT	Participants — Manufacturing • Materials • Management Period — 1-2 months Point — Ensure workers never hide unnecessary items.
⬇	
2 DISTINGUISHING RED TAG ITEMS	Stock — Raw materials • Parts • Products Facilities — Machines • Equipment • Jigs and tools • Molds • Carts • Desks Spaces — Floor • Shelves • Storage
⬇	
3 FIXING RED TAG STANDARDS	Clarify standards for unnecessary items: e.g. "NO TAG" for items to be used within the next month; "TAG ON" for items not to be used within the next month.
⬇	
4 PRODUCTION OF RED TAGS	It's important that everybody can see them at a glance! • A4 size red paper • Include name of item, quantity, reasons, etc.
⬇	
5 ATTACHING TAGS	• Don't let people directly concerned attach them! • Listen to no excuses! • Be strict about it! • Attach tags to any doubtful item! • The number of tags indicates checking efficiency not failure!
⬇	
6 DEALING WITH RED TAG ITEMS & EVALUATION	Stock — List unnecessary stock, by dividing into dead stock and sleeping stock. Equipment — Move or eject any items which hinder the implementation of 5S activities.

15

2. What do we attach red tags to?

- Red tag anything that's not needed!
- In manufacturing departments that means checking stock, machines, equipment, particular locations such as shelves, etc.
- In clerical departments it includes documents, stationery and machines.
- However, you should never ever red tag people, even if you are sometimes tempted to!

☞ Checkpoints

1. **Stock**................ Raw materials, parts, work-in-progress, component parts, finished products.

2. **Facilities**............ Machines, equipment, jigs, tools, cutting tools, molds, fittings, carts, pallets, lifts, work tables, vehicles, desks, chairs.

3. **Locations**........... Floors, shelves, rooms.

4. **Documents** .... Notices, circulars, minutes, office reports, drafts, quotations, memos, numerical data.

5. **Machines**........... Copy machines, word processors, personal computers, facsimile machines, shredders.

6. **Fittings** .... Folders, binders, document files, cabinets, lockers, boxes for materials, desks, chairs.

7. **Stationery**.......... Pencils, propelling pencils, ball-point pens, felt-tip pens, erasers, clips, memo pads.

8. **Others**............... Slips, name cards, books, magazines, newspapers, plans, pamphlets.

One red tag per item

Collect all tagged items together

3. Deciding the standards for red tags

"It's wasteful to throw things away!"
"It was so much trouble for me to make these things!"
"We might possibly use these later!"
- These are very common and natural reactions to the idea of getting rid of unnecessary items, whether it be at home or in the factory.
- It's very important to decide on clear standards for "what is really needed" and "what is not needed" to overcome these arguments.

Checkpoints: Standard production patterns

1. **Pattern A** — Retain any items to be used within the NEXT MONTH, according to the production schedule. Tag everything else.

Plant A (Ordinary)

NOW

| 1 month | 2 months | |

Needed   Not needed = red tags

2. **Pattern B** — Retain any items to be used within the NEXT WEEK, according to the production schedule. Tag everything else.

Plant B (Strict)

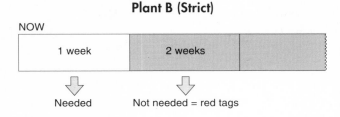

3. **Pattern C** — Tag any items which have not been used in the PAST MONTH, according to the production schedule. They are not needed.

Plant C (Repetitive Production)

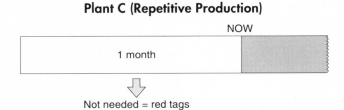

4. Making red tags

> - The tags are red to make them stand out and draw attention to factory "grime."
> - They also remind people of safety considerations.
> - Any material will serve the purpose as long as it is striking.

Checkpoints

 1. Make the red tags prominent:
- Red paper
- Red adhesive tape
- Clear plastic covers for tags
- Red round seals

2. Write reasons and notes on the tag:

3. Information on tags:
- Classification .... Stock, machines, etc.
  - Raw materials, work-in-progress, products, equipment.
  - Jigs, tools, molds, fittings, etc.
- Item Identification .. Names, numbers.
- Quantity .... Number of items with red tags attached.
- Reason .... In the case of stock, unnecessary items, defective products, non-urgent items, etc.
- Section.................... Section responsible for control of tagged items.
- Date .... The date when the tag was attached.

RED TAG

Classification	1. Raw material 5. Machine/Equipment 2. Work-in-progress 6. Mold • Jig 3. Component part 7. Tool • Fitting 4. Finished product 8. Other		
Name of Item			
Order number			
Quantity/Value	_____ items	Value per item:	Total:
Reason	1. Unnecessary 4. Leftover material 2. Defective 5. Unknown 3. Non-urgent 6. Other		
Section responsible	_____ Dept. _____ Section _____ Group		
Action	1. Eliminate 2. Return 3. Move to red-tag storage 4. Store separately 5. Other	Completed	
Date	Tag attached Year____Month____Day____	Action taken Year____Month____Day____	
Reference No.			

©JIT Management Laboratory Co., Ltd.

5. Attaching red tags

"Shouldn't workers at the workplace attach them?"
- No. Attaching tags requires a second person's viewpoint.
- That means that someone other than the operator should attach the tags.
- Put red tags on any doubtful item!

Checkpoints

 1. Person responsible ... Managers or members of staff not directly responsible for that particular machine or work station.

2. Attachment period ... 1 day, or 2 days if necessary.

3. Attitude .... • Workers will believe everything is necessary!
   • Look at situation with a very critical attitude!
   • Be a red tag demon!

Red tags attached

6. Action and evaluation

> ■ The next step is to clarify WHY red tags have been attached, and decide on the appropriate course of action to take.

Checkpoints

 1. Stock............... Divide tagged items into four categories:

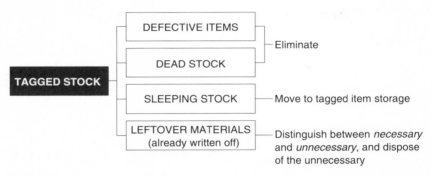

2. Equipment......... Eliminate anything which interferes with improvement activities.

Stock

Equipment

PROCESS 2:
FIXING STORAGE PLACES (ORGANIZING)

2-1. Cleaning Before Organizing

- The first thing required is some work with brooms and rags to get the dirt off.
- *Organizing* means *standardization of storage*, but standardizing cannot start until everything's clean.

Checkpoints

 1. Eliminate unnecessary items first.

2. Clean very dirty places and empty spaces from which unnecessary items have been removed.

If in doubt, eliminate!

Do cleaning together

2-2. Creating an Address Grid

> ■ Does your factory have a proper *address grid*?
> ■ Every machine and every storage place needs its own address.

Checkpoints

1. Use pillars to divide the floor area into zones.

2. Regard horizontal divisions as *districts* and the vertical divisions as *sub-districts*.

3. Use letters (A,B,C......) and numbers (1,2,3......).

4. Use large, clear labels.

Create addresses like grid references on a map

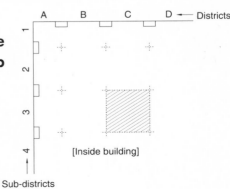

2-3. Adding Color to the Workplace: A Painting Strategy

1. Floors

- All work areas should be painted with colors which do not promote stress.
- Rest areas should use the most relaxing colors.
- The floors can be painted once the layout has been carefully considered and everything fixed in position.

Checkpoints

 1. Use different colors for floor areas depending on function. Work areas need appropriate colors for working, rest areas need more relaxing colors.

	AREA	COLOR	NOTES
FLOORS	Work Areas	Green	
	Aisles	Orange	Fluorescent paint
	Rest Areas	Blue	
	Warehouses	Gray	

2. If the floor is not level, do repairs first.

3. Reduce curves in aisles to an absolute minimum.

A rest area designed for comfort (South Korea)

**A pleasant workplace begins
with clean and attractive floors**

2. Drawing floor lines

■ Once the floor color has been decided, it is possible to divide it into sections with lines.

Checkpoints

 1. Although paint is normally used, tapes or acrylic sheets are also suitable.

2. Start drawing lines to delineate aisles and work areas.

3. Decide whether traffic will move on the right or the left. (If possible, follow the normal situation on roads.)

4. Use broken lines for exits and entrances.

5. Use a *tiger pattern* for areas where caution is required.

TYPE		COLOR	WIDTH (cms)	NOTES
Dividing lines		Yellow	10	Solid lines
Exits/Entrances		Yellow	10	Broken lines
Door openings		Yellow	10	Broken lines
Traffic flow lines		Yellow		Arrows
Tiger pattern		Black & Yellow		Stripes
Storage space lines	Work-in-progress	White	5	Solid lines
	Work tables	White	5	Corner lines
	Ashtrays, etc.	White	3	Broken lines
	Defective items	White	5	Solid lines

• Basic Rules: "Never walk on yellow lines or step over them!" "Dividing lines are lifelines!"

2-4. Begin with Dividing Lines

1. Dividing lines

- Dividing lines are those which delineate aisles and working areas. Although they are usually yellow, it is also possible to use white.

Checkpoints: How to paint dividing lines

1. Use only straight lines.

2. Make all lines clear and obvious.

3. Minimize corners.

4. Avoid right angles at corners.

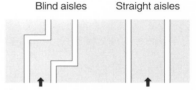

Blind aisles · Straight aisles

- Difficult to see ahead
- Accidents likely

- Easy to see ahead
- Smooth movement

**There are many points to notice in this example:
entrances/exits, traffic flow lines, stop marks, angled corners, etc.**

2. Entrance/exit lines

- You should never walk on yellow lines or step over them.
- Entrances and exits should be created and marked.
- These are known as *entrance/exit lines*.

Checkpoints

 1. Dividing lines use solid lines, entrance/exit lines use broken lines.

2. Safety is the first consideration for the positioning of entrance/exit lines.

3. Make sure everyone fully understands the system.

Safety is a prime consideration

3. Door opening lines

- Most of us have experienced a door suddenly swinging open in our face at some time or other.
- It's important to know which way the door is likely to open.

Checkpoints

 1. Always think from the point of view of people who use the door.

2. Safety at all times is the prime consideration.

3. Use labels saying "DON'T OPEN THIS DOOR SUDDENLY!"

4. Lines on the floor point out the danger.

No problem here even if the door opens suddenly

4. Traffic flow lines

- Left or right?
- The important thing is to fix a traffic flow policy for walking and driving within the factory.
- This is a major way to avoid collisions and accidents.

Checkpoints

1. Use yellow or white arrows.

2. Leave regular gaps between arrows and add corner arrows as necessary.

3. Don't forget to mark stairs and steps.

Decide on the rule for traffic flow, left or right

5. Tiger patterns

- A *tiger pattern* consists of oblique black and yellow stripes, and serves as a warning signal.

Checkpoints

1. Make a list of dangerous places:

   - Anything sticking out into the aisle
   - Anything crossing the aisle
   - Danger of electric shock
   - Overhead danger
   - Anywhere you need to watch your step
   - Stairs or steps
   - Cranes
   - Moving machines or equipment

2. Mark tiger patterns very clearly:

   - Paint   • Tape

3. Nothing should be left sticking out into the aisles.

Clearly indicate the danger point

33

6. Storage space lines

- Space for storage of any kind should be clearly demarcated with lines.
- Prime examples are work tables and areas used to store work-in-progress.

Checkpoints

 1. Make a list of all areas used for storing work-in-progress.

2. Make a list of other storage areas, such as work tables and storage positions for extinguishers, carts, etc.

3. White is the color most often used. However, red or another outstanding color can be used to indicate defective items.

Decide the normal storage position and mark it

Don't hide defective items

2-5. Implementing a Signboard and Labeling Strategy: Visual Organization

1. A signboard strategy at the workplace

- There are many types of signs, signboards and labels for use in the workplace.
- We should set them up in this order:
  factory → workplace → line → process.

Checkpoints

1. Signs should be large and clear.

2. Colors should be used to differentiate factories, workplaces and lines.

3. Major signboards should be clearly visible from the entrance to the factory.

Workplace signboard

Line signboard

2. Detailed sign strategy

■ The strategy for signs extends down to small details, such as process signs, machine signs, and even name-tags on workers' uniforms.

Checkpoints

 1. All signs should be as big and clear as possible.

2. Identify all machines by name and number.

3. Use a variety of colors.

Process signs

2-6. The 3 Keys to Organizing

1. Organizing is a form of standardization

■ If you were asked "What is *Organizing*?", what would you reply?

Checkpoint: One keyword and 3 points

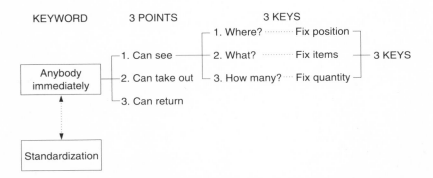

To organize
is
to standardize storage

2. The 3 Keys are the basic rules for storage

- The three basic points to remember about storage: WHERE?, WHAT? and HOW MANY?
- Labeling should be done in a way that makes sure anybody can understand the answers to these questions!

Checkpoints

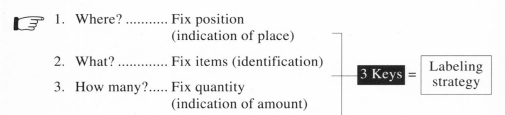

1. Where? .... Fix position (indication of place)
2. What? .... Fix items (identification)
3. How many?..... Fix quantity (indication of amount)

3 Keys = Labeling strategy

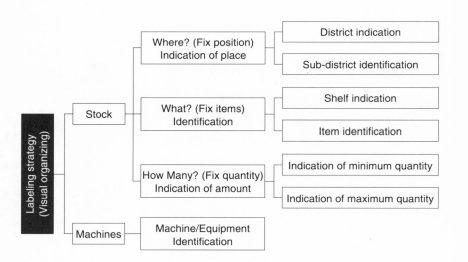

3. Fixing position

■ How should we fix the position for all stock items?

Checkpoints

1. Identify distinct *blocks* of shelving, using letters (A, B, C. . .) or any appropriate designation.

2. Each *block* should be further divided into columns (*streets*) and rows (*house numbers*).

3. The street numbering can use either letters (A, B, C...) or numbers (1, 2, 3...), from left to right.

4. Numbers are recommended for the *house numbers*, from top to bottom.

5. The top of the shelf is not a storage place so it has no number.

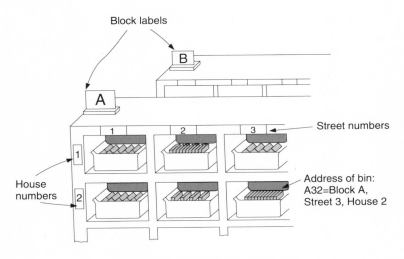

Labeling of fixed positions

4. Fixing items

■ Is it easy to understand exactly what items are stored in the storage place?

Checkpoints

 1. Item identification — label on the item stored there (i.e. ID number or name)

2. Shelf indication — label to show what item is stored on that shelf (should be the same as item identification).

3. If the item identification label is designed to be removable, it can serve as a *kanban* for inventory and ordering.

4. The shelf indication label should also be removable to facilitate storage layout adjustments.

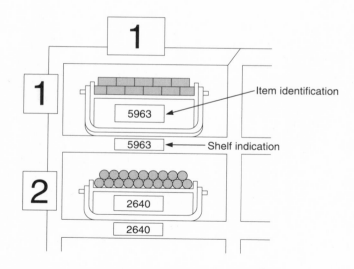

Item identification and shelf indication

5. Fixing quantity

> ■ Is it possible to say exactly how many stock items are left at a glance, rather than having to say "Well, around....?"

Checkpoints

1. Limit the size of storage places and shelves.

2. Clearly indicate minimum and maximum stock quantities:

   - maximum — red
   - minimum — yellow

3. A mark is better than numbers.

4. Quantity should be clear at a glance, without the need for counting.

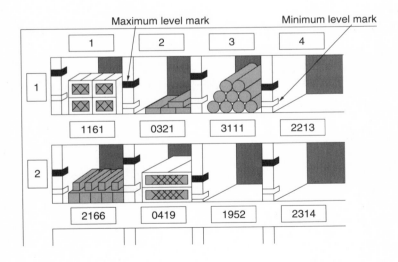

Indication of quantity (fixing quantity)

6. Signs for storage of work-in-progress

- If detailed signs are attached to the storage places for work-in-progress and outsourced items, you can immediately recognize how much of what is where.
- For work-in-progress, both the previous and the next processes should be clearly indicated.

Checkpoints

1. Storage place name • Code—name and code of storage place

2. Product name • Code—name and code of stored product

3. Previous process • Next process—indication of processes

4. Max/ Min—maximum and minimum stock quantity

5. Person responsible—name of person responsible

Storage Place Name		Storage Place Code	
Product Name		Product Code	
Previous Process		Next Process	
Quantity	MAX MIN	Person Responsible	

42

2-7. Jigs and Tools: Changing from a Closed to an Open Storage System

■ Can you see your jigs and tools when they are in their storage place?
■ If not, then it's likely that the storage will soon get very messy!

STEP • I

Checkpoints

1. If jigs and tools are stored inside lockers, boxes or drawers, they cannot be seen (*closed storage system*).

2. Jigs and tools should be visible at a glance.

3. Storage for easy visibility is known as an *open storage system*.

Closed storage system

Open storage system

43

2-8. Jigs and Tools: Functional Organization

- Jigs and tools can easily end up all over the floor or on top of machines if their storage places are not fixed in detail.

Checkpoints

 1. Sort out all the jigs and tools in use at the workplace and make a list.

2. Decide on place of storage and container.

3. A tilted board is an ideal container.

4. Classify all jigs and tools into clear groups ready for immediate use.

Grouping of jigs and tools

PROCESS 3:
CONSOLIDATING DAILY CLEANING PROCEDURES (CLEANING)

3-1. Order of Cleaning

> ■ The purpose of cleaning is to get rid of all dust and dirt and keep the workplace spotless.
> ■ Do you clean your workplace every day?

Checkpoints

1. Decide what to clean.

2. Decide who is in charge of each cleaning task.

3. Decide on cleaning methods.

4. Prepare cleaning tools and equipment.

5. Implement cleaning.

Treat machines and other equipment as family treasures!

3-2. Cleaning Targets

> ■ There are three broad categories to target for cleaning: storage areas, equipment, and surroundings.

Checkpoints

1. Storage areas ..... warehouses, shelves for work-in-progress, shelves for jigs and tools, etc.

2. Equipment .... machines and equipment of all types, transporters, jigs and tools, etc.

3. Surroundings ..... aisles, windows, meeting rooms, toilets, etc.

Storage areas

Work areas

Surroundings

1. Storage areas

> - This category includes a wide range of items and places.
> - So what exactly should be cleaned?

Checkpoints: Storage areas — what to clean?

 1. Products warehouses

2. Parts warehouses

3. Materials warehouses

4. Storage areas inside the factory for work-in-progress

5. Parts storage areas

6. Line storage areas

7. Machine processing storage areas

8. Shelves for jigs and tools

Could you find what you wanted here?

2. Equipment

- You have to take care of your own machine and keep your tools clean and orderly all the time.
- This is the viewpoint of the professional.

Checkpoints: Equipment — what to clean?

1. Machines
2. Equipment
3. Welding tools
4. Tools
5. Cutting tools
6. Measuring tools
7. Molds

8. Wheels
9. Transporters
10. Work tables
11. Cabinets
12. Desks
13. Chairs
14. Fittings

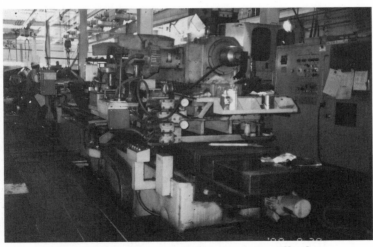

Keep your machines clean and you'll always know what condition they're in!

49

3. Surroundings

- If the place where you work every day is covered in grime, you can easily get depressed.
- Make it clean and comfortable, and keep it that way!

Checkpoints: Surroundings — what to clean?

 1. Floors

2. Work areas

3. Aisles

4. Walls

5. Pillars

6. Ceilings

7. Windows

8. Rooms

9. Electric lights

**Think how good you feel after a haircut!
That's the feeling we're after.**

3-3. Cleaning Responsibilities

- Who is responsible for cleaning the break rooms?
- Is cleaning done every day or every other day?
- Who is responsible for what?

Checkpoints

1. Draw up a cleaning responsibility map.

2. Create a cleaning schedule.

3. Clearly display the map and the schedule.

Example of a cleaning responsibility sheet:

Cleaning Responsibility	
Cleaning Area	A3 – A6
Person Responsible	Thomas Jones
Cleaning Times	Mon - Fri 08:25 - 08:30

1. Cleaning responsibility map

- Responsibility is best allocated by dividing the workplace into small areas.
- Everybody should clean up the workplace together.

Checkpoints

 1. Draw a map of the workplace.

2. Divide the map into small areas for cleaning.

3. Allocate people to take charge of each area.

4. Display the map in a conspicuous place.

Example of a cleaning responsibility map:

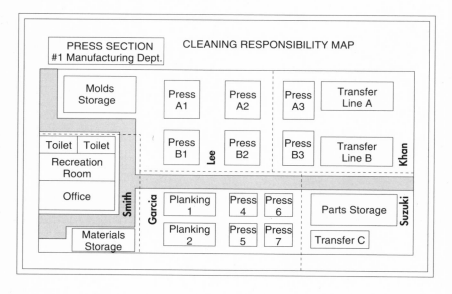

2. Cleaning schedule

- Before setting a schedule for cleaning, make a list of all the cleaning activities.
- A shift system is generally a good idea, especially for the cleaning of communal areas.

Checkpoints

 1. Communal areas: meeting rooms, recreation rooms, library, etc.

2. Allocation: from amongst the users, decide on the person in charge.

3. List the cleaning work, sort out, and allocate the daily schedule.

4. Make the schedule and display it. The person on duty is identified by a *duty tag*.

A typical duty schedule

Break Room Duty Schedule						
Day	Name	Vending machines	Floors	Tables	Ashtrays	Wash basins
Mon	Wilson					
Tue	Atkin	✓	✓	✓	✓	✓
Wed	Szabo					
Thu	Goldman					
Fri	Copperfield					

3-4. Fixing Cleaning Methods

> ■ Once you've decided WHO is doing the cleaning, and WHEN, you can decide just HOW the cleaning should be done.

Checkpoints

 1. Make daily 5-minute cleaning a habit.

2. List necessary cleaning tools and equipment according to the cleaning procedures.

3. Clarify use of all the cleaning tools and equipment, and their order of use.

4. Apply *Organizing* to all cleaning tools and equipment.

Don't forget to clean in the corners and out-of-the-way places!

1. 5-minute cleaning

- Five minutes may sound too short a time in which to achieve anything worthwhile.
- But if the cleaning is done efficiently, you'll be surprised how much can be done!

Checkpoints

1. Five minutes should be spent on cleaning every morning.

2. Limit the cleaning time to 5 minutes.

3. Decide exactly what kind of cleaning should be done during the 5 minutes each morning, and specify this on the schedule.

4. Clean efficiently!

2. Cleaning order

- If you just hear the word "cleaning," nobody knows what to do first or where to start.
- Five minutes can soon pass while you're wondering what to do!

Checkpoints

 1. Decide on the order of cleaning jobs to be done . . .
   a) every day
   b) not every day

2. Make a daily cleaning check list.

3. Display the list at the workplace and use for checking.

Example of a daily cleaning schedule:

CLEANING SCHEDULE		Dept. Sect.	Manufacturing #1 Press Section			
		Person	George Smith			
No.	LOCATION	MON	TUE	WED	THU	FRI
1.	Break Room	O	O	O	O	O
2.	Locker Room	O			O	
3.	Office		O		O	
4.	Materials Storage			O		
5.						
6.						
7.						
8.						
9.						

3. Cleaning tasks and cleaning tools

> ■ Once you've fixed the cleaning tasks by deciding what items need to be cleaned, the next thing is to make a list of all the tools for the job.

Checkpoints

1. List the cleaning tasks for each person.

2. Decide on suitable tools for each task:

   Brooms
   For preliminary sweeping of chips or filings on the floor.
   Mops
   Basically used for wiping floors.
   Dust cloths/Rags
   - Use dust cloths for work tables, office desks, machines, etc.
   - Use wet rags if there is a lot of dirt and dust.
   - For polishing or removing oil use dry dust cloths or rags.

3-5. Preparation of Cleaning Tools

■ Cleaning tools should always be stored in a place with easy access!

Checkpoints

 1. Prepare all the tools needed for the cleaning tasks.

2. Indicate the required number of each tool at each storage place, and put the tools in place.

3. Make sure all the storage places have easy access.

YES:	NO:
Only the tools you need located where you need them	All tools of the same type stored together

3-6. Implementation of Cleaning

- Now it's time to start cleaning!
- Just see how clean you can get things in 5 minutes!

Checkpoints

1. Push a broom
2. Use a dust cloth $\Big\}$ — get into the habit!

3. Remember:

- Sweep in all the corners, along the edges of walls, and around pillars.
- Sweep/wipe dust and dirt off walls, windows, doors, etc.
- Remove pollutants completely...dirt, dregs, waste, scraps, broken fragments, filings, oil, stains, rust, dust, sand, paint, etc.
- Clean until you get down to the original surface.
- If the dirt won't come off easily, use cleaning detergents, polishing powder, etc.
- Everybody should help with the cleaning.
- Machines and equipment should be cleaned by the people who use them.

First of all, grab a dust cloth!

PROCESS 4:
MAINTAINING A SPOTLESS WORKPLACE (STANDARDIZING)

4-1. A Tidy Workplace at All Times!

- The workplace can be kept clean and tidy if everyone puts in a little effort.
- The secret is in remembering three NO principles:
  - NO unnecessary items
  - NO mess
  - NO dirt

Checkpoints

1. Are there any unnecessary items around you?

2. Are all jigs and tools immediately accessible?

3. Is cleaning done every morning?

4. Is clearing up done every day after work?

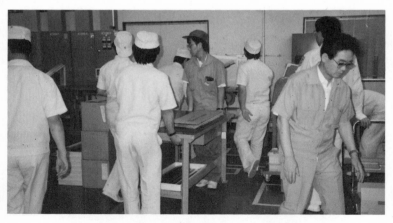

Act promptly and act together!

4-2. Check Unnecessary Items First

1. Checkpoints for unnecessary items

■ The idea here is to check if there are any unnecessary items remaining after application of the *Red Tag Tactic.*

CHECKLIST FOR UNNECESSARY ITEMS AT THE WORKPLACE		Dept.				
		Checker			Date:	/ /
NO.	CHECKPOINT	CHECK		ACTION (Inc. deadline)		
		YES	NO			
1	Are there any unused items in storage?					
2	Is there anything in the aisles which is not in use?					
3	Are there any unnecessary machines?					
4	Are there any unnecessary items on or under the shelves?					
5	Are there any unnecessary items around or under the machines?					
6						
7						
8						
9						
10						

2. List items for scrapping

- It's amazing how many unnecessary items emerge.
- Through application of the *Red Tag Tactic*, the average factory produces at least 10 truckfuls of scrap!

Checkpoints

1. Equipment and stock are the company's assets.

2. Individual employees must not dispose of anything without permission.

3. Make a list of all unnecessary stock items or pieces of equipment.

4. Every item must be included on the list.

5. Disposal takes place only after discussion with those in charge of financial matters.

List of unnecessary stock items

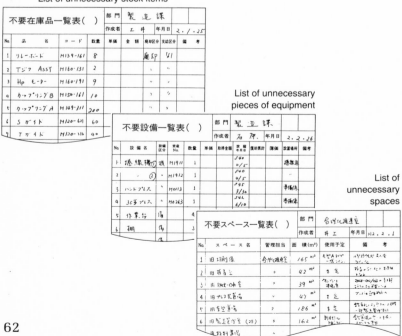

List of unnecessary pieces of equipment

List of unnecessary spaces

4-3. Checking Storage (Organizing)

1. Checkpoints for storage

- Are all stock items, jigs and tools properly organized?
- Let's look at some storage checkpoints.

NO.	CHECKPOINT	CHECK YES	NO	ACTION (Inc. deadline)
	WORKPLACE CHECKLIST Dept. / Checker / Date: / /			
1	Is storage of products fully organized?			
2	Have the 3 Keys been applied to the storage of assembly parts?			
3	Have the 3 Keys been applied to the storage of parts and materials?			
4	Have more than 80% of floor lines been drawn?			
5	Do jigs and tools have an open storage system?			
6	Are all jigs and tools fully organized?			
7	Can all stored molds be seen at a glance?			
8				
9				
10				

2. Appraisal lists

- Of all the 5S steps, Organizing is the most far-reaching.
- Re-checking is vital, and an appraisal list is useful for this.
- If there are more than 30 NO answers on the list, then it's necessary to go back to the start of Step 1, Organizing.

Checkpoints:

Usage
The list includes points concerning the organization of jigs, tools and stock items and is very useful as a check list for the appraisal of Organizing activities.

Explanation of main items

1. Dept./Process .... Fill in the department and the particular process to which Organizing is being applied.

2. Checker .... The name of the person who does the checking.

3. Class .... Classification of objects for Organizing (e.g. Jigs and Tools, Safety, etc.).

4. Checkpoints .... Questions to determine progress and effectiveness of Organizing.

5. Check .... To be checked by the person making the tour of inspection:

   - YES = point is sufficiently covered

   - NO = point is not covered and action is required

6. Countermeasure
   /Improvement Ideas, etc. (Inc. deadline)
   .... If any item is checked NO, it is necessary
                               to fill in an appropriate countermeasure or
                               suggestions for improvement made by the
                               workers at the workplace, together with the
                               deadline for action.

Example of a completed checklist:

ORGANIZING CHECKLIST			Dept. Process			
			Checker		Date: / /	
Class	No.	Checkpoint	Check		Countermeasure/ Improvement Ideas (Inc. deadline)	
			Yes	No		
STOCK	1	Are there 3 Keys signs at all storage places?				
	2	Can you see quantity indicators at a glance?				
	3	Are items stored perfectly: horizontally, vertically, at right angles, in parallel?				
	4	Is storage 3-dimensional to make the best use of space?				
	5	Is a *first-in, first-out* system being used?				
	6	Are there partitions or cushions to keep items apart?				
	7	Is dust being effectively avoided?				
	8	Is the floor free of items stored directly on it?				
	9	Is storage of defective items set?				
	10	Are storage areas for defective items clearly labeled?				
JIGS & TOOLS	11	Can all defective items be seen at a glance?				
	12	Is storage for jigs and tools set?				
	13	Are there 3 Keys signs at all storage areas?				
	14	Are names or code numbers attached to all jigs and tools?				

Class	No.	Checkpoint	Check		Countermeasure/ Improvement Ideas (Inc. deadline)
			Yes	No	
	15	Are jigs and tools in regular use kept near the workplace?			
	16	Are items kept in appropriate sets?			
	17	Is storage done according to the work schedule?			
	18	Are all jigs and tools stored at the places indicated in the work manual?			
	19	Is it easy to spot items stored in the wrong place?			
	20	Is improper storage corrected immediately?			
	21	Is sharing of items fully implemented?			
	22	Have all possible measures been taken to reduce the number of jigs and tools?			
JIGS & TOOLS	23	Has attention been paid to how easy it is to return items?			
	24	Are items in regular use stored within 10cms. of the place of use?			
	25	Is all other storage less than 10 steps away?			
	26	Is all storage sufficiently high so that it is not necessary to bend down to take out items?			
	27	Is hanging storage used fully?			
	28	Can items be returned without having to look?			
	29	Are the dimensions of storage devices right for fumble-free return?			
	30	Has an effort been made to avoid constant changing of jigs?			
	31	Is organizing done by shape?			
	32	Is organizing done by color?			

Class	No.	Checkpoint	Check		Countermeasure/ Improvement Ideas (Inc. deadline)
			Yes	No	
CUTTING TOOLS	33	Are tools in regular use kept near the operator?			
	34	Are tools used infrequently stored for communal use?			
	35	Are tools kept in appropriate sets?			
	36	Are measures taken to avoid tools touching each other?			
	37	Are corrugated sheets used for the bottom of drawers?			
	38	Are tools in drawers aligned from front to back?			
	39	Is stacking of grinding wheels always avoided?			
	40	Are measures taken to avoid rust on cutting edges?			
MEASURING TOOLS	41	Are dust and dirt kept out of storage facilities?			
	42	Are the 3 Keys in operation at storage places?			
	43	Is the deadline for realignment or replacement clearly indicated?			
	44	Are micrometers and dial gauges stored in a vibration-free place?			
	45	Are cushions used to avoid vibration?			
	46	Are measures taken to protect plug gauges and nut gauges?			
	47	Are squares and test bars hanging or otherwise protected to avoid deformation?			
OIL	48	Is the oil storage/drum/oiler lubrication point system organized by color?			
	49	Is all oil of the same type stored together?			
	50	Are there 3 Keys signs at all storage areas?			

STEP · I

Class	No.	Checkpoint	Check		Countermeasure/ Improvement Ideas (Inc. deadline)
			Yes	No	
SAFETY	51	Are all aisles free of obstructions?			
	52	Are long boards, etc., always stored flat or fully upright?			
	53	Are there proper supports for objects liable to fall over?			
	54	Are all tall piles of items guaranteed not to collapse?			
	55	Are all piles of items kept to a reasonable height?			
	56	Are hoods or covers used for all rotating parts?			
	57	Are all dangerous areas fenced off?			
	58	Are all danger signs clear and easily visible?			
	59	Can all fire extinguisher signs be seen from everywhere?			
	60	Are all fire extinguishers properly stored?			
	61	Are there any obstacles in front of fire hydrants or emergency water tanks?			
	62	Are there stop marks at all crossings, etc.?			
		TOTAL			

General Comments

4-4. Checking for Dust and Dirt (Cleaning)

1. Cleaning checkpoints

> ■ Running a finger along a windowsill will soon show just how clean the workplace is!

DUST-FREE/DIRT-FREE CHECKLIST		Dept.			
		Checker		Date: / /	
NO.	CHECKPOINT	CHECK Yes	No	ACTION (Inc. deadline)	
1	Are the items and shelves in the products warehouse free of dust?				
2	Are parts, materials, and shelves free of dust?				
3	Are machines free from dirt and excess oil?				
4	Is the area around machines free from chips and oil?				
5	Are all aisles and floors shining?				
6	Has a paint strategy been implemented?				
7	Is the factory floor free of iron chips and scraps?				
8					
9					
10					

2. Cleaning checklists

■ Let's think about remedial action.

Checkpoints:
Usage

The list includes checkpoints regarding stock items, equipment and spaces for the appraisal of *Cleaning* activities.

Explanation of main items

1. Department .... Fill in the department and the particular process to which *Cleaning* is being applied.

2. Checker.................... The name of the person who does the checking.

3. Class .... Classification of objects for *Cleaning* (e.g. Stock, Spaces, etc.).

4. Checkpoints .... Questions to determine progress and effectiveness of *Cleaning*.

5. Check....................... To be checked by the person making the tour of inspection:

   • YES = cleaning is done effectively

   • NO = cleaning is not done effectively and some action is required

6. Action (Inc. deadline) If any item is checked NO, it is necessary to fill in an appropriate action to be taken, together with the date by which action will be taken.

Example of a completed checklist:

CLEANING CHECKLIST			Dept. Process			
			Checker		Date:	/ /
CLASS	NO.	CHECKPOINT	CHECK Yes	CHECK No	ACTION (Inc. deadline)	
STOCK	1	Has dust and dirt been removed from all products, parts and materials?				
	2	Has all rust that appeared on parts after cutting or cleansing been removed?				
	3	Has all dirt been removed from stock shelves?				
	4	Has all dirt been removed from storage areas for work-in-progress?				
	5	Has all dirt been removed from transfer pallets for stock or work-in-progress?				
EQUIPMENT	6	Has all dust and oil around machines and equipment been removed?				
	7	Has all water, oil and dirt underneath machines and equipment been removed?				
	8	Has all dust, grime and oily dirt been removed from machines and equipment?				
	9	Have all oily or dirty fingerprints been removed from the sides of machines and equipment or control panel covers?				
	10	Has all dirt on glass parts of oil levels and pressure gauges been removed?				
	11	Have all lids and covers been taken off to get at internal grime and dust?				
	12	Has all dust, grime and dirt been removed from air pipes and wires?				
	13	Has all dust, grime and oil been removed from switching devices?				
	14	Has all dust and dirt stuck on phototubes been removed with a soft cloth?				
	15	Has oily grime and dirt been removed from every nook and cranny with wet rags?				
	16	Has all dirt and dust been cleaned from jigs, tools and cutting blades?				
	17	Has all oily grime been removed from molds?				
	18	Has all dirt and dust been removed from measuring tools?				

71

| CLASS | NO. | CHECKPOINT | CHECK | | ACTION |
			Yes	No	(Inc. deadline)
	19	Has all sand, soil, dust and dirt been removed from floors and aisles?			
	20	Has all water and oil been removed from floors and aisles?			
	21	Has all dust and grime been removed from walls, windows, and windowsills?			
	22	Have all dirty fingerprints and dust been cleaned from windows?			
	23	Has all dust and grime been removed from ceilings and roof-beams?			
SURROUNDINGS	24	Has dust been removed from all light bulbs and fluorescent tubes?			
	25	Has dust been removed from all lampshades, light covers, etc.?			
	26	Has all dirt and dust been removed from shelves, work tables, etc.?			
	27	Has all oil and dirt been removed from steps and stairs?			
	28	Has all dirt and filth been removed from the bottom of pillars, walls, corners, etc.?			
	29	Have all empty cans and general dirt around the building been removed?			
	30	Has all the filth been removed from outside walls and detergent used to clean them, etc.?			
		TOTAL			

General Commentsmeasuring tools?

PROCESS 5:
VISUAL CONTROL IN THE WORKPLACE
(TRAINING & DISCIPLINE)

5-1. Visual Control: The First Step in Training & Discipline

- A healthy workplace is one that always welcomes constructive criticism.
- Giving and taking constructive criticism is one basis of the Training & Discipline step of 5S.
- The ideal is to create a workplace where problem points can be recognized at a glance, so that remedial action can be taken.

VISUAL CONTROL CHECKLIST		Dept.				
		Checker			Date: / /	
NO.	CHECKPOINT	CHECK		ACTION (Inc. deadline)		
		YES	NO			
1	Are the 3 Keys in operation in the products warehouse?					
2	Are the 3 Keys in operation for parts and materials?					
3	Can you distinguish unnecessary items in the factory at a glance?					
4	Are all the floor lines working effectively?					
5	Is the color of the floor correct?					
6	Are the 3 Keys in operation for jigs and tools?l					
7	Are the 3 Keys in operation for molds?					
8	Is the workplace floor shining?					
9	Are all the machines shining?					
10	Is everybody sticking to the rules?					

5-2. A 5S Photo Display

- The factory should have changed a lot since the photos were taken back at the beginning of Step I.
- The time has come to hold an exhibition of *before* and *after* 5S photos.

Checkpoints

 1. Take *After* 5S photos.

2. It's important to take the photos from the same position and angle as the *Before 5S* photos.

3. Put the photos together on a 5S *Results Table*.

4. Add comments on 5S results.

5. Decide on the display area and period for the display and inform all staff.

6. Use a location everyone visits regularly, such as the dining room.

Display the photos where everyone will see them!

5-3. 5S Slogans

- The whole company should be involved with 5S.
- A way to get everyone interested is to request at least one idea for a 5S slogan from every member of the company.

Checkpoints

1. Enlist the cooperation of everybody in the company.

2. Form a selection committee to pick out the best slogans.

3. Put slogans on hanging banners, badges, ribbons, etc.

4. Display slogans at conspicuous places.

5. Change slogans every week or even daily.

5-4. STEP I Radar Chart

> - Now is the time for full evaluation of the effectiveness of 5S checking according to the type of workplace.
> - Results should be posted up and prizes can be given as an incentive for further improvement.

Checkpoints

 Usage

Separate checklists can be prepared according to the type of workplace (e.g. office, factory floor). They give a detailed evaluation of the effectiveness of 5S in each workplace. Results can be used as the basis for a "5S Contest."

Explanation of major items

1. 5S .... Divided into Clearing Up (*Seiri*), Organizing (*Seiton*), Cleaning (*Seiso*), Standardizing (*Seiketsu*), and Training & Discipline (*Shitsuke*).

2. Marks...................... There is a grading from 0-4 marks:

   0 = Very bad
   1 = Bad
   2 = Average
   3 = Good
   4 = Very good

Examples of completed checklists:

5S CHECKLIST (OFFICE)			Section	Checker			
			Marks /100	Previous marks /100	Date: /	/	

5S	NO.	CHECKING ITEM	EVALUATION CRITERIA	MARKS				
				0	1	2	3	4
CLEARING UP (/20)	1	Lockers	No irrelevant reference materials, such as documents, drawings, meeting materials, etc.					
	2	Desks	No excess pieces of equipment or reference materials on desks or in drawers.					
	3	Visual control	Irrelevant items or documents can be identified at a glance.					
	4	Standards for disposal	Standards are fixed for disposal of documents and equipment.					
	5	Exhibits	Displays are up-to-date, tidy and well-balanced.					
ORGANIZING (/20)	6	Storage labels	Labeling of lockers and equipment allows immediate identification.					
	7	Labels for documents and equipment	Everything is clearly identified.					
	8	Ease of use	Storage is designed for ease of use.					
	9	Orderly storage	Everything is stored in a fixed place.					
	10	Aisles and display areas	All dividing lines and bulletin boards are clearly indicated.					
CLEANING (/20)	11	Floor	The floor is clean.					
	12	Dust and dirt	Windows, windowsills and shelves are clean.					
	13	Cleaning responsibilities	There is a rotation or shift system for cleaning.					
	14	Wastebaskets	There is a system for getting rid of dirt and waste paper.					
	15	Habitual cleaning	Sweeping and dusting are regarded as habitual activities.					

5S	NO.	CHECKING ITEM	EVALUATION CRITERIA	MARKS				
				0	1	2	3	4
STANDARDIZING (/20)	16	Ventilation	The air is clean, odorless and free of cigarette smoke.					
	17	Lighting	The angle and intensity of illumination are appropriate.					
	18	Uniforms	Nobody is wearing a dirty uniform.					
	19	Environment	The general environment is good, including color, air, lighting, etc.					
	20	The first 3 Steps	There is a system for maintaining Clearing Up, Organizing and Cleaning.					
TRAINING & DISCIPLINE (/20)	21	Clothing rules	The rules are adhered to.					
	22	Interaction of people	There is a pleasant general atmosphere, people exchange greetings, etc.					
	23	Meeting times and break times	Everyone makes an effort to be punctual.					
	24	Telephone manners	Everyone states their business clearly, politely and succinctly.					
	25	Rules and regulations	All rules and regulations are strictly observed.					
Total		Check dispersal of marks (total for each column)						

5S CHECKLIST (PRODUCTION DEPT.)			Section	Checker			
			Marks /100	Previous marks /100	Date: / /		

5S	NO.	CHECKING ITEM	EVALUATION CRITERIA	MARKS				
				0	1	2	3	4
CLEARING UP (/20)	1	Parts or materials	No unnecessary stock items or work-in-progress.					
	2	Machines and equipment	All machines and pieces of equipment are in regular use.					
	3	Jigs, tools and molds	All jigs, tools, molds, cutting tools and fittings are in regular use.					
	4	Visual control	All unnecessary items can be distinguished at a glance.					
	5	Standards for disposal	There are clear standards for eliminating excess.					
ORGANIZING (/20)	6	Storage labels	There are labels to indicate different *districts* and *sub-districts*.					
	7	Labels shelves and stored items	All shelves and items in storage are labeled clearly.					
	8	Quantity indicators	There are clear indications of maximum and miminum stock quantities.					
	9	Dividing lines	Dividing lines are all clear and all painted white.					
	10	Jigs and tools	Storage of jigs and tools is well organized for ease of extraction and return.					
CLEANING (/20)	11	Floor	The floor is always clean and shining.					
	12	Machines	Machines are kept clean.					
	13	Cleaning and checking	Cleaning and checking are regarded as the same thing.					
	14	Cleaning responsibilities	There is a rotation or shift system for cleaning.					
	15	Habitual cleaning	Sweeping and wiping are regarded as habitual activities.					

5S	NO.	CHECKING ITEM	EVALUATION CRITERIA	MARKS				
				0	1	2	3	4
STANDARDIZING (/20)	16	Ventilation	The air is clean and odorless.					
	17	Lighting	The angle and intensity of illumination are appropriate.					
	18	Work clothes	Nobody is wearing dirty or oil-stained work clothes.					
	19	Avoidance of dirt	Emphasis is placed on avoiding the accumulation of dirt.					
	20	The first 3 Steps	There is a system for maintaining Clearing Up, Organizing and Cleaning.					
TRAINING & DISCIPLINE (/20)	21	Clothing rules	The rules are adhered to.					
	22	Interaction of people	There is a pleasant general atmosphere, people exchange greetings, etc.					
	23	Meeting and smoking	Everyone strives to be punctual and observe smoking regulations.					
	24	Rules and procedures	All rules and work procedures are acknowledged and respected.					
	25	Observation of rules	All rules and regulations are strictly observed.					
Total		Check dispersal of marks (total for each column)						

STEP I
5S Radar Chart

Section	
Date	

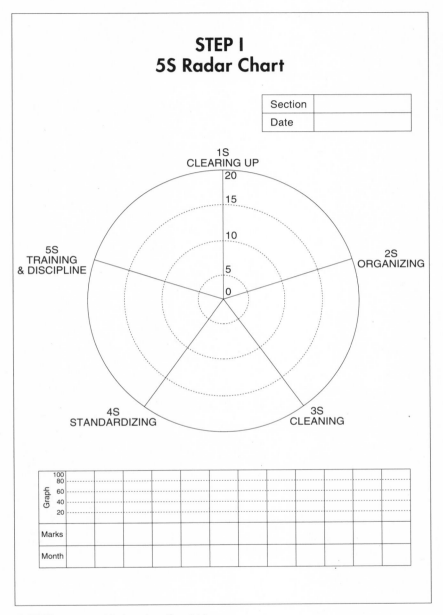

©JIT Management Laboratory Co., Ltd.

FINALLY:
CAN YOU SEE THE IMPROVEMENTS?

1. A much cleaner factory

- What do you think of the *before* and *after* photos below?
- As you can see, this factory was originally very dirty and untidy.
- Thanks to the application of 5S, it now looks totally different and a huge space has been made available.

Checkpoints

 1. 5S photos and 5S checklists are a valuable record of improvements in the factory.

2. This is just the start of 5S activities.

3. Don't become complacent!

4. Strive to make 5S activities habitual.

Empty space

Materials storage area

2. Progressing from STEP I to STEP II

- Now you should have a clean factory.
- But is it possible to keep it that way?
- Only if you make it a habit!

Checkpoint: Move on to STEP II

STEP

MAKING A HABIT OF 5S
(Effective 5S)

PREPARATION:
PHOTOGRAPHING THE NEW LOOK AT THE WORKPLACE

- The first thing to do is compare how clean your workplace
  has become compared with what it was like before
  you started 5S.
- Then you can move on from STEP I and advance even further
  with STEP II.

Checkpoints

Taking photographs from the same position serves as proof of what
has been achieved.

**Before 5S
(Insufficient cleaning
and cluttered aisles)**

**After 5S
(Daily 5-minute 5S
provides the much-
needed cleaning)**

PROCESS 1:
CONTROLLING STOCK LEVELS (CLEARING UP)

1-1. Applying the Red Tag Tactic to Stock

■ Once maximum and minimum stock levels have been established, more precise control of stock is possible.

■ Then we can gradually work to decrease inventories without disrupting production. As before, the key is to use red marks (lines, labels or tags) to indicate maximum levels, and yellow marks to indicate minimum levels.

Checkpoints

1. Use clear labels and signs on all stock.

2. Use *red marks* to indicate maximum stock levels.

3. Gradually lower the red marks (maximum level).

4. This will result in a stronger inventory system that allows production to be carried out with less stock on hand.

"Can you tell the maximum stock level at a glance?"

1-2. Inspection by the Red Tag Patrol Team

- The red tag patrol team makes a tour of inspection at least once a month and evaluates each section with respect to the disposal of unnecessary items.

Checkpoints

 1. The patrol team is made up of representatives from each workplace.

2. There should be a regular tour of inspection every month.

3. The patrol visits every section in the factory.

4. The evaluations given by the patrol are announced.

"It still isn't quite right...."

1-3. Red Tags on Unnecessary Stock

1. Controlling the quantity purchased

- Items not in use are not the only items which need tagging.
- There should also be red tags on anything which will certainly not be used within a certain period (e.g. one month).

Checkpoints

 1. Reduce the quantity ordered at any one time.

2. Increase the number of deliveries of supplies.

3. The maximum and minimum stock levels should be clear at a glance.

4. Checking for excess stock on the spot.

"Which item is overstocked?"

2. Controlling quantity of outside orders

- The placing of outside orders is, of course, part of the general process.
- What is essential is helping the outside source to be more flexible in responding to changes in the work environment.
- When storage of products ordered from the outside is reduced, problems in the production flow become more visible.

Checkpoints

 1. The maximum stock level (red mark) for outside orders should be clear at a glance.

2. Supplies over the maximum level should also be obvious.

3. Regularly reduce the maximum stock level.

4. Create "lines" in the factory for outside orders.

Maximum stock level (red mark)

"Why is the tag attached to a thread?"

3. Controlling quantity for stores

- Storage areas for parts in transit between processes are called *stores*.
- Is inventory control also being applied to stores?
- Does the downstream process communicate to the upstream process its desire to cut back on the quantity of items sent to it?

Checkpoints

1. The maximum stock level should be clear at a glance.

2. Regularly reduce the quantity.

3. Make transit containers smaller (e.g. pallets, boxes).

4. Make changes and improvements in the upstream process.

Changing the system from a maximum quantity of 4 boxes down to 3 boxes

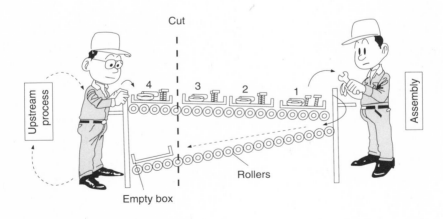

4. Controlling line inventory

- On the assembly line, it's important to reduce the number and size of movements workers have to make.
- Tools and parts should be located conveniently, and, if possible, in one place, and the number of parts should be reduced.

Checkpoints

 1. How many minutes' worth of parts are stored at the line side?

2. Reduce the present quantity by 50%:
   e.g. 4-hour storage (half a day) → 2-hour storage

3. Clearly indicate the maximum inventory.

4. Make the containers more compact to reduce the maximum quantity by half.

5. Ensure there is a first-in, first-out system (FIFO).

"Rhythm is the heart of assembly"

5. Controlling inventory around heavy equipment

- There are always two types of storage areas for processing machines and equipment.
- One is storage before processing.
- The other is storage after processing.
- Are the 3 Keys used to decrease inventory both before and after processing?

Checkpoints

1. Are the 3 Keys working?
   - Fixed position .... delineated by floor lines
   - Fixed items .... "Pre-processing storage area XXX"
     "Post-processing storage area XXX"
   - Fixed quantity .... Indicate quantity contained in each box or on each pallet.

2. Reduce the size of containers by half (e.g. boxes, pallets).

3. Implement a no-lift, no-crane system.
   - Eliminate pallets and use carts for moving everything.
   - Eliminate the use of wires suspended from crane hooks.

"Don't let storage become an obstruction!"

PROCESS 2:
MAKING IT EASY TO USE AND RETURN THINGS
(ORGANIZING)

2-1. Marking Reference Materials with an Oblique Line

- Can you see at a glance whether files are out of place?
- Can you detect disorder from a distance?
- Oblique lines can be used to show if any file is out of order.

Checkpoints

 1. Put numbers on the spines of all files and binders according to an established ordering system.

2. Organize by color, using colored labels, etc.

3. Draw oblique lines across the files.

"What a difference a line makes!"

2-2. Marking Everything (Organizing by Outlining Shapes)

1. Jigs and tools: outlining shapes

- Do you know exactly what types of jigs and tools are being used now?
- Can you tell at a glance where you should return specific jigs and tools?

Checkpoints

1. Put names and numbers on all jigs and tools.

2. Put corresponding names and numbers on all storage positions.

3. Outline the shapes of jigs and tools at their precise storage positions.

4. Differentiate groups by color.

"Outlines show what goes where"

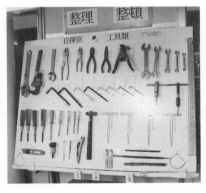 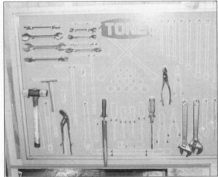

2. Placement marks for ash stands, extinguishers, etc.

■ Is the proper marking organization in use for all ash stands in smoking areas, fire extinguishers, etc.?

Checkpoints

 1. Use either solid white or yellow broken lines for placement marks.

2. Outline the shape of ash stands, extinguishers, etc.

3. Put names on the placement marks even if there is nothing stored there at present.

4. Remember that the 3 Keys are the basis.

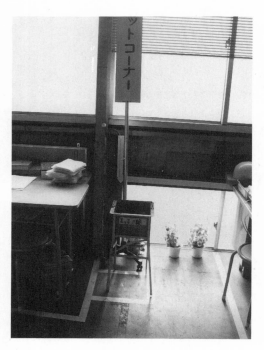

"The 3 Keys are essential, even for minor things"

2-3. Adding Color to the Workplace (Organizing by Color)

1. Materials storage

> ■ Do you sometimes produce defects because of mistakes with the quality of materials?
> ■ Such defects can be completely avoided by using color organization.

Color grouping

The idea is to ensure that all items in the same group are the same color. This makes it very easy to identify materials at a glance.

Checkpoints

1. Divide materials into groups.

2. Assign a color to each group.

3. Paint the color on the edge of the materials and the appropriate storage.

4. Remember the 3 Keys.

"Paint the end of the rods, and there'll be no confusion"

97

2. Lubricating oil

> - Most factories use many different types of lubricating oil, and oil containers are often moved from workplace to workplace.
> - Can you guarantee that you are always using the correct type of lubricating oil?

Checkpoints

 1. The 3 Keys must be strictly applied.

2. Assign a color for each type of oil.

3. Ensure that all storage drums, oilcans and oilers are painted the same color.

4. Attach a seal in the same color to every lubrication point.

"Always the right lubricant for the job!"

3. Jigs and tools

- Color should also be used to make it possible to identify jigs and tools at a glance.

Checkpoints

In cases where each machine requires different jigs and tools.

1. Allocate a different color for each machine.

2. Paint jigs and tools for each machine in the appropriate color.

3. Also implement organizing by outlining shape.

"Can you immediately find the item you need?"

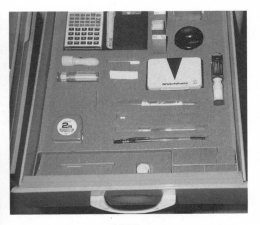

YES

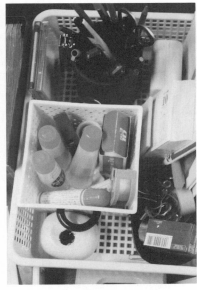

NO

4. Molds

■ Is it easy to tell with which machine any particular mold is used?

Checkpoints

 1. Assign a color to each machine and piece of equipment.

2. Group molds according to which machines they are used with.

3. Assign the same color to all items in one group.

4. Use the same color for associated molds, machines and storage places.

5. If you change the storage place for molds, all you have to do is use a sign in the appropriate color at the new storage place.

"Can you tell which molds belong in the same group?"

2-4. Creating Production Lines

- The creation of lines involves a lot more than just finding a suitable layout for pieces of equipment.
- Also included is the sorting out of ideas and items according to the requirements of the downstream process.

Checkpoints

1. First of all, it's important that everyone involved fully understands the work that has to be done by the line, and their own role.

2. Sort out individual tasks and their sequence to create a work flow.

3. Set up the equipment, parts storage, and jigs and tools in such a way that the line will work efficiently.

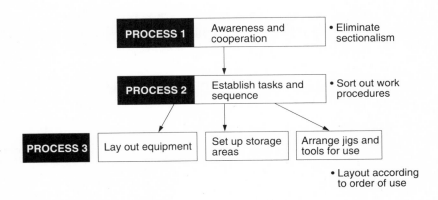

PROCESS 1 — Awareness and cooperation — • Eliminate sectionalism

PROCESS 2 — Establish tasks and sequence — • Sort out work procedures

PROCESS 3 — Lay out equipment | Set up storage areas | Arrange jigs and tools for use

• Layout according to order of use

2-5. Storage for Production Lines

1. Parts storage

- There are two ways of organizing parts storage: by type of part or by the product in which it will be used.
- An example of the first is storing all bolts together, regardless of where they will be used.
- This kind of storage tends to increase the amount of movement involved when taking out the required parts.

Checkpoints

 1. Storage by type .... This method of allocation makes it easier to replace stocks of parts as required.
This makes it more suitable for individual production because it allows closer control of ordering and inventory.

2. Storage by product ... This method is much more suitable for a production line, because it makes it much easier to move the products on to the next process.
It also makes it easier to find the appropriate materials and parts, and reduces wasteful movement.

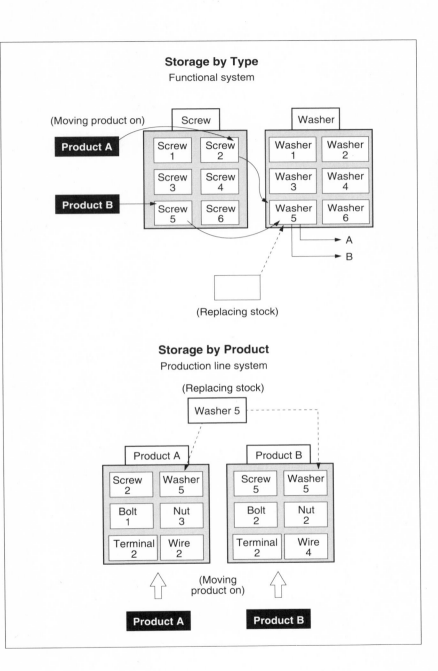

Storage by Type
Functional system

(Moving product on)

Product A

Product B

Screw

Screw 1
Screw 2
Screw 3
Screw 4
Screw 5
Screw 6

Washer

Washer 1
Washer 2
Washer 3
Washer 4
Washer 5
Washer 6

A
B

(Replacing stock)

Storage by Product
Production line system

(Replacing stock)

Washer 5

Product A

Screw 2
Washer 5
Bolt 1
Nut 3
Terminal 2
Wire 2

Product B

Screw 5
Washer 5
Bolt 2
Nut 2
Terminal 2
Wire 4

(Moving product on)

Product A

Product B

STEP · II

103

2. Implementing line marshaling

■ Is mixed flow production possible with the way you organize parts storage at present?
■ Implement a marshaling system by setting up parts storage closer to the line.

Checkpoints

 1. Switch to mixed flow production from lot production.

2. For parts supply, change from lot supply to marshaling supply.

3. For effective marshaling, put parts storage nearer to the line.

4. Establish storage by product.

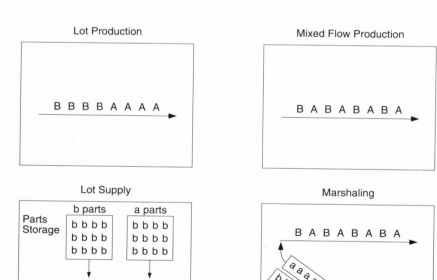

3. The vital factor in mixed flow production is parts supply in the correct sequence

- Ideally speaking, there is nothing better than an exclusive line.
- But these days mixed flow production is essential because of the increase in the number of types of products.
- Parts supply is the biggest factor when switching from lot production to mixed flow production.

STEP · II

Checkpoints

1. Decide the sequence of products in the production flow.

2. Decide the sequential order of parts required to match the flow of production.

3. Ensure there is a first-in, first-out (FIFO) supply system.

Flow-oriented parts supply

Type-oriented parts supply

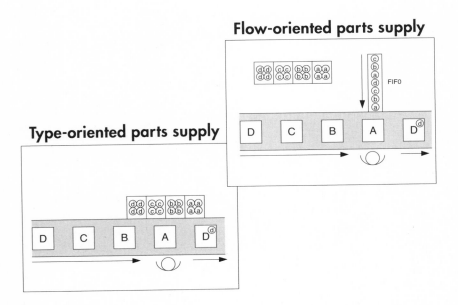

4. Storage of tools beside each machine

> ■ How long does it take to do a set-up during a changeover?
> ■ The ideal is to make one-time set-up possible within 100 seconds by storing set-up tools beside each machine.

Checkpoints

 1. Abolish centralized storage of tools.

2. List the particular tools needed for each machine.

3. Supply extra tools as required.

4. Set the required tools beside each machine.

5. Apply the three principles of:

Easy to See, Easy to Get At, Easy to Return.

Storage beside each machine

106

5. Tools storage according to sequence of work operations

- Look carefully at your tools storage.
- How is it organized?
- Storage is generally done by type: e.g. box wrenches, allen wrenches, etc.
- But is that the way you divide up your work?

Checkpoints

Tools storage according to the work flow is known as "creating a line for tools"

1. Change from centralized storage to storage beside each machine.

2. List the sequence of work operations.

3. List all tools necessary for the work process.

4. Lay out tools in the same sequence as the operations in the work process.

5. Vital points for tools storage are *Easy to Get At* and *Easy to Return*.

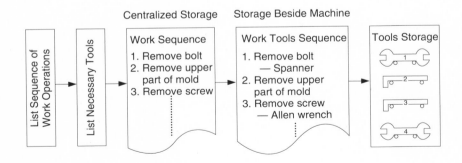

107

PROCESS 3:
MAKING CLEANING AND CHECKING HABITUAL
(CLEANING)

3-1. Checking as Part of Cleaning

- There is usually no time to do checking separately from daily cleaning.
- The secret is to make checking a part of daily cleaning.

Checkpoints

 1. Cleaning every morning should become a habit (5-minute cleaning).

2. Cleaning should include checking.

3. During cleaning, point out every checking point and say "OK!"

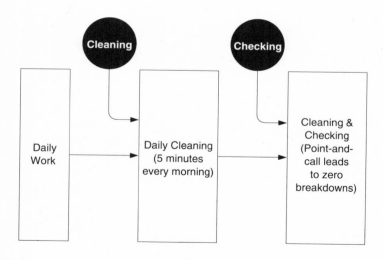

3-2. Procedure for Cleaning and Checking

- The aim is to achieve zero breakdowns, zero operation errors, and zero short stoppages through effective cleaning and checking.
- A procedure is required for implementation.

Checkpoints
Procedure for cleaning and checking

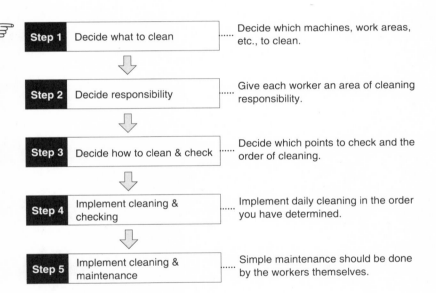

Step 1	Decide what to clean	Decide which machines, work areas, etc., to clean.
Step 2	Decide responsibility	Give each worker an area of cleaning responsibility.
Step 3	Decide how to clean & check	Decide which points to check and the order of cleaning.
Step 4	Implement cleaning & checking	Implement daily cleaning in the order you have determined.
Step 5	Implement cleaning & maintenance	Simple maintenance should be done by the workers themselves.

STEP · II

3-3. Deciding What to Clean and Check

> - Basically, everything connected with the production process should be cleaned and checked.
> - Most important, of course, are all the machines and pieces of equipment.

Checkpoints

1. Floors	6. Cutting tools	11. Cabinets
2. Machines	7. Measuring tools	12. Desks
3. Equipment	8. Molds	13. Chairs
4. Jigs	9. Transporters	14. Fittings, etc.
5. Tools	10. Work tables	

"All set up to break down!"

3-4. Deciding Responsibility for Cleaning and Checking

- It's no good if only certain areas of the factory are cleaned thoroughly and others are ignored.
- It is vital to assign responsibility for cleaning and checking for every area.

Checkpoints

1. Decide the cleaning and checking area for each section or group.

2. Assign areas of cleaning responsibility to each worker.

3. Display a map of the factory indicating all areas and who is responsible for each one.

4. Use "Cleaning and Checking Area" labels on pillars and floors.

"Make it clear who is responsible for cleaning"

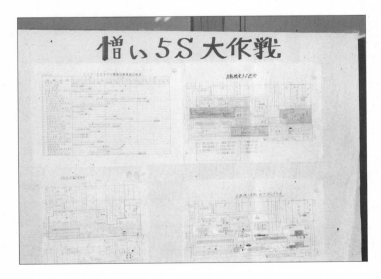

3-5. Decide on Cleaning and Checking Procedures

1. Obvious problem points

- The first thing to do is look at the actual situation in the workplace to find out how much dirt there is, if there are any leakages, damage, etc.
- Then it's possible to make a list of problem points and consider what action to take.

Checkpoints

 1. List every problem point found on machines and equipment.

2. "Why did it occur?" Investigate reasons for occurrence.

3. Decide on countermeasures.

4. Prepare a "Cleaning & Checking Points" checklist from the viewpoint of problem points to be removed and avoided in future.

Cleaning & Checking Points: Problem Checklist

No.	PROBLEM	POINTS	COUNTERMEASURE
1	Rubbish, dirt	Dust, dirt, grime, rubbish, rust, chips, waste, filings, other dirt	Cleaning
2	Oil	Leakage, stains, no oil, oil shortage, wrong oil type	Lubrication Replace with new oil Cleaning/Repair
3	Temperature/ Pressure	Temperature too high, temperature too low, pressure too high, pressure too low, coolant temperature abnormality, off-standard control devices	Repair/Restoration
4	Looseness	Loose bolts, detached bolts, loose nuts, detached nuts, slack belts, welding detachments	Extra tightening Replacement Repair/Restoration
5	Damage	Broken hoses, torn hoses, broken meters, broken glass, broken switches, unraveled wires, broken arms, loose rotating parts	Replacement Repair/Restoration

2. Functional checkpoints

- We also need checkpoints for the operational functions of each machine and piece of equipment so that problems can be dealt with swiftly.

Functional Checkpoints

Item (Order)	No.	Problem Point	Countermeasure			
			Clean	Lubricate	Replace	Repair
Oil Pressure 1. Operating oil reservoir 2. Operating oil pump 3. Control valve 4. Operating cylinder	1. 2. 3. 4. 5. 6. 7. 8. 9. 10. 11. 12. 13. 14.	There is dust and dirt around the lubrication intake. Gages show there is insufficient oil. You cannot clearly see the level indicator and level meter. Inadequate seal on the oil-pressure reservoir. The inside and bottom of the tank are dirty. The operating oil is dirty. The oil is running low. The wrong type of oil is in use. The suction filter is dirty. The pump is making an abnormal sound. The pump is generating abnormal heat. Oil is leaking from the control valves. Oil is leaking from flanges (pipes). Oil is leaking from the operating cylinder (hydraulic cylinders).				
Air Pressure 1. 3-piece air set 2. Control valve 3. Operating cylinder 4. Exhaust port	15. 16. 17. 18. 19. 20. 21. 22. 23. 24. 25.	There is dust and dirt inside the air filter. The oil inside the oiler is dirty. The oil level in the oiler is too low/high. The drip level inside the oiler is too low/high. Air is leaking from the control valves. Air is leaking from the flanges (pipes). The control valve is making an abnormal sound. The control valve lock nuts are loose. Air is leaking from the actuator (air cylinders). Installation screws are loose (air cylinders). The exhaust port is blocked.				
Lubrication 1. Lubrication intake 2. Tank 3. Pipes 4. Lubrication parts	26. 27. 28. 29. 30.	There is dust and dirt around the lubrication intake. Indicators show there is insufficient oil. You cannot clearly see the level indicator or level meter. Inadequate seal on the reservoir. The inside and bottom of the tank are dirty.				

113

Item (Order)	No.	Problem Point	Countermeasure			
			Clean	Lubricate	Replace	Repair
Lubrication 1. Lubrication intake 2. Tank 3. Pipes 4. Lubrication parts	31. 32. 33. 34. 35. 36. 37.	The oil inside the tank is dirty. There is oil leakage from the reservoir and the flanges. The oil is running low. The wrong type of oil is in use. The pipe is blocked. There is dust and dirt around the lubrication parts. The lubrication equipment is dirty.				
Mechanical System Moving parts Sliding parts Rotating parts	38. 39. 40. 41. 42. 43. 44. 45. 46. 47. 48. 49.	There is dust and dirt around the sliding parts. There are cracks, dents, or differences in level around the sliding parts. The sliding parts are making an abnormal sound. There is dust and dirt on the vanes. Rotation of the vanes is erratic. The vanes are making an abnormal sound. Fixing screws are loose. The V-belt and chain are loose. The pulley is making an abnormal sound. The gear has too much play. The table and bed are scratched or pitted. The table and bed are not level.				
Electricals	50. 51. 52. 53. 54. 55. 56. 57. 58. 59. 60. 61. 62. 63.	The indicator light is dirty. The indicator lamp pilot light is not working properly. The door or lid of the control panel is damaged. The seal and rubber on the edge of the door and lid are damaged. Wires inside the panel are broken, unraveled or frayed. The joint is dirty or damaged. The printed board is bent, not properly fixed or dirty. Fixing screws are loose. The tape heads on the NC machine are dirty. Switches are dusty or dirty. Phototubes are dusty or dirty. The timer or relay is being operated beyond the manufacturer's specifications. The ground is not firmly connected. The ground is not properly insulated.				
Jigs and Tools Cutting Tools Measuring Tools	64. 65. 66. 67. 68. 69. 70.	Jigs and tools are dirty or covered in dust. Jigs and tools are faulty in some way. Jigs are not set accurately. Cutting tools are cracked. Cutting tools don't cut properly. Micrometers, dial gauges, etc., are dirty. Measuring tools are not set accurately.				

3. Making a cleaning and checking list

> ■ Now we can make a cleaning and checking list for each machine.

Checkpoints

 1. Decide the machines which need a cleaning and checking list.

2. List up all points to be checked.

3. Make a monthly cleaning and checking list.

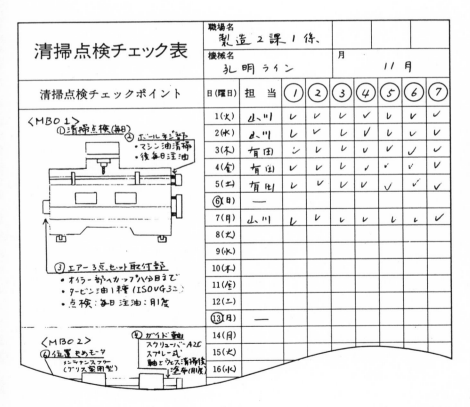

115

3-6. Implementation of Cleaning and Checking

- Once the cleaning and checking list has been prepared, there's no time to waste!
- You should get on with implementing it right away.

Checkpoints

 1. Display the cleaning and checking list.

2. If there are too many checkpoints to be covered, assign them to different days.

3. Implement 5-minute cleaning and checking every morning.

4. Attach seals or tags to all points which need checking to make them clear at a glance.

5. It's a good idea to paint footmarks on the floor to show the correct place to stand to do the check.

6. During actual checking, point at each item to be checked and confirm aloud that it is in the proper condition ("Point-and-call").

"What are those footmarks for?"

PROCESS 4:
Maintaining a Spotless Workplace
(Standardizing)

4-1. Are There Standards for the Elimination of Unnecessary Items?

- You should never get to the point where you feel ovewhelmed by clutter in the workplace.
- Instead, you should establish standards for the elimination of unnecessary items from your immediate surroundings.

Checkpoints

1. Are the 3 Keys working properly?

2. Are there standards for elimination for each workplace and each storage area?

   - Example 1   Standards for eliminating chips
   - Example 2   Are there marks to show maximum quantity levels?
   - Example 3   How long are items kept beside the line?

3. Who will remove things if anything goes beyond the *standard for elimination*?

4. You should make it a habit not only to eliminate items, but also to make sure all unnecessary items have red tags attached and are removed as soon as possible from the workplace.

"Is it clear when you have to empty the basket?"

4-2. Can Order Be Restored Quickly?

> - What happens if any cleaning tools are left lying around or jigs and tools are not returned to storage after use?
> - There should be a system so that something is done about it quickly.

Checkpoints

 1. Are the 3 Keys fixed for stocks, jigs and tools, etc?

2. Does everyone who comes across messy storage immediately take action to remedy the situation?

3. Does the department manager or section chief regularly patrol the workplace?

4. Is there a 5S inspection patrol team?

5. Is proper storage taken seriously in the workplace?

"Be strict on the spot about a messy workplace"

4-3. Is Dirt Cleaned Up Immediately?

> ■ Are the floor and machines ever left dirty?
> ■ If so, then cleaning has not yet become a habit!

Checkpoints

1. Are all the cleaning areas clearly differentiated?
2. Is the person responsible for each cleaning area fixed?
3. Is daily cleaning implemented?
4. Is a cleaning checklist in use?
5. Are dustbins, cans for filings, and boxes of chips emptied regularly?
6. Has an inspection patrol team been set up?
7. Are frank opinions and advice freely exchanged?

"Hmm, it's amazing how quickly it gets dirty again!"

4-4. Are the First Three Steps of 5S Being Practiced Fully?

■ To what extent have the principles of Clearing Up, Organizing and Cleaning become habitual?
■ It's time to check.

Checkpoints

☞ 1. CLEARING UP

	YES	NO
• Are *standards for elimination* and *red tag standards* applied to each workplace and every type of part?	☐	☐
• Are you following the standards for clearing up?	☐	☐

2. ORGANIZING

	YES	NO
• Can storage disarray be seen at a glance for both stock and tools?	☐	☐
• Is any messy storage taken care of immediately?	☐	☐

3. CLEANING

	YES	NO
• Is everything kept so clean that the least bit of dirt is noticed immediately?	☐	☐
• Is there a regular cleaning schedule?	☐	☐

PROCESS 5:
MAINTAINING STANDARDS THROUGHOUT THE COMPANY
(TRAINING & DISCIPLINE)

5-1. Becoming a Leader Who Can Give Constructive Criticism

1. Discipline has to begin with strict standards

In the top-rank manufacturing factories, there are always people who are strict and good at maintaining discipline.
Who are they in your factory?

Checkpoints

1. Visual controls help to ensure discipline and teamwork:

   - Are demarcation lines drawn properly?
   - Are signs and labels well displayed?
   - Are the 3 Keys applied to all storage?

2. Are standards clear and unambiguous...

   - With regard to safety?
   - With regard to quality?
   - With regard to work, etc?

5S SLOGANS

Category	No.	Slogan	Comments
The need for 5S	1.	Even the factory enjoys a good bath.	Factories are like people ... they feel better when they're cleaned up.
	2.	Don't just set up change, change setup!	Improve setup to do multiple flow production.
	3.	Zero defects: first discipline, then prevention of mistakes.	How to achieve zero defects.
	4.	The more the waste, the greater the cost.	Cutting costs through zero waste.
	5.	"The delivery's on its way" won't do in the factory	The target is zero delays with delivery dates.
	6.	Caution saves lives. Tidiness means safety.	Zero injuries–safety is a vital consideration.
	7.	Trust must be earned!	Improvement in trust comes from completing 5S implementation.
	8.	Service begins in the factory.	The factory is the base to provide customer service via products.
5S in general	9.	Do you really need it?	Improvement of efficiency begins with organization.
	10.	Organizing standardizes storage.	Proper organization eliminates time spent on searching.
	11.	First of all, grab a broom!	Cleaning is the base for quality improvements.
	12.	Survival of the cleanest!	Standardization generates enthusiasm and a can-do feeling.
Clearing up	13.	A cheerful greeting is a good way to start discipline.	5S begins and ends with discipline.
	14.	Red tags show up the grime!	The *Red Tag Tactic* is visual organization.
	15.	Like a bull seeing red!	The whole company is involved with the *Red Tag Tactic*.
	16.	Do we want it or don't we?	Standards for unnecessary items should be clear.
	17.	Go on! Be a red tag demon!	Attach red tags to everything which needs one.
Organizing	18.	Good organizing means easy return.	Clarify where, what and how many?
	19.	Use it a lot? Have it to hand!	Fix storage according to frequency of use.
	20.	Which address for which part?	An address indicates the exact location.
	21.	More discipline, less disorder.	Good clearing up comes from habit.
	22.	Label it!	Put signs and labels on processes and machines.

Category	No.	Slogan	Comments
Organizing	23.	So, what's wrong?	The *3 Keys*: fix position, fix items, fix quantity.
	24.	FIFO, the only way to go!	The basic rule is FIFO (first-in, first-out).
	25.	Remember, things have to be moved!	Decide on storage to increase transportation efficiency.
	26.	Keep the line in mind.	It's easy to take out parts if they're stored by product.
	27.	A place for defects, a place for products	Provide separate storage for perfect products and defective products.
	28.	Take it back!	Make sure jigs and tools are always returned.
	29.	Too many tools and jigs?	Is it possible to eliminate any jigs and tools?
	30.	Fewer tools, less trouble	Go for consolidated use of jigs and tools.
	31.	Set-up without moving?	The point of storage should be near the point of use.
	32.	Find the right shape!	Organization by shape.
	33.	Do you have to look?	Returning to the original location without even looking.
	34.	Simple release ... that's organizing!	Returning to the original location without even thinking.
	35.	Blunt blades, bad products.	Storing cutting tools individually.
Cleaning•Standardizing• Training & Discipline	36.	The procedure is the standard.	Standards should be incorporated in the actual work procedure.
	37.	Constant breakdowns — inadequate cleaning.	Cleaning is checking.
	38.	Dirt on the floor means defects galore.	The problems of the factory are found on the floor.
	39.	Always clean is better than always cleaning.	Why is dust and dirt generated?
	40.	Commitment — the glue that holds 5S together.	"Who cares?" is a taboo phrase in the workplace.

123

2. Giving constructive criticism

- Constructive criticism is really a sign of commitment.
- Basically a boss who cannot criticize constructively is a failure as a manager.

Checkpoints

People good at giving constructive criticism can do so because they are committed to:

 1. **The workplace**
They're committed to their work.

2. **Products**
They're committed to maintaining the quality of the products the company produces.

3. **Training**
They're committed to training their subordinates.

3 facets of the effective supervisor

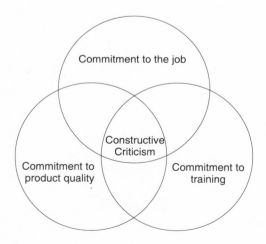

3. On the spot correction

■ The basis of good correction is to do it on the spot whenever there is some sign of disorder, and to make sure it's done in a reasonable way.

Checkpoints

Correction should always be specific and helpful, based on the 4W1H principles

1. WHAT & WHERE? Give correction ....
   At the actual place • In the actual situation • With the actual items

2. WHEN & WHY? Give correction ....
   Immediately • Without hesitation •In response to a specific problem

3. HOW? Give correction ....
   Thoroughly • Thoughtfully • Constructively

Giving correction based on 4W1H

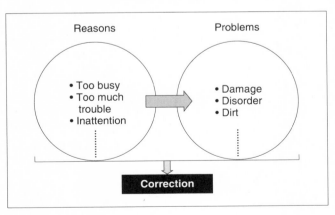

5-2. Leaders Should Also Be Ready to Accept Criticism

1. How to respond to criticism

> ■ The best way to improve is to take seriously the criticisms directed at you.

Checkpoints

Response to criticism is also based on 4W1H principles

 1. WHAT & WHERE? Respond ....
At the actual place • In the actual situation • With the actual items

2. WHEN & WHY? Respond ....
Immediately • Without hesitation •In response to a specific problem

3. HOW? Respond ....
Thoroughly • Thoughtfully • Willingly

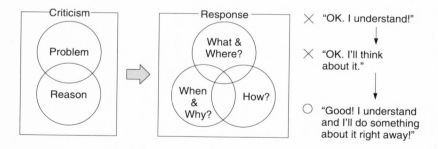

2. The leader is a model for the team

> ■ Workers at the workplace can learn a lot from the dynamic interchange between people who know that constructive criticism is important for learning.

Checkpoints

1. The head of a department and the head of a section are both company leaders, but the group leader is the person who has the most effect on the actual workplace.

2. People who are serious about their work should be able to give and accept criticism with a spirit of cooperation.

3. If discipline is clearly lacking in the workplace, bosses should give constructive criticism to group leaders rather than to individual workers.

4. The group leader is the person responsible for creating the general character of the workplace.

5. The group leader's commitment will have a positive effect on the workers.

Developing discipline

5-3. STEP II Radar Chart

- The theme of STEP II is "Making a Habit of 5S!" Have you succeeding in doing that yet?
- You can check on your progress by using this "STEP II 5S Checklist"

Checkpoint: Fill in the radar chart to evaluate progress

5S	STEP II 5S Checklist / Checking Item	Section / Checker		Class / Date			
		Marks					
	Checking Item	Unsatis-factory	Not too bad	Average	Better than average	Sufficient	Total
Clearing Up	1. The Red Tag Tactic has been implemented.	0	1	2	3	4	
	2. There are no unnecessary items at the workplace.	0	1	2	3	4	
	3. Maximum quantity levels are clear at a glance.	0	1	2	3	4	/20
	4. Quantity control is in effect for storage.	0	1	2	3	4	
	5. There are no extra quantities in the work area.	0	1	2	3	4	
Organizing	6. Office organization and clearing up have been implemented.	0	1	2	3	4	
	7. Organization of jigs and tools by shape is in effect.	0	1	2	3	4	
	8. Organization of materials, oil, jigs and tools by color is in effect.	0	1	2	3	4	/20
	9. Parts for mass production are stored by product.	0	1	2	3	4	
	10. Lines for jigs and tools have been created.	0	1	2	3	4	
Cleaning	11. Cleaning has become habitual.	0	1	2	3	4	
	12. Cleaning includes checking.	0	1	2	3	4	
	13. Responsibility for each cleaning area has been determined.	0	1	2	3	4	/20
	14. A checklist for cleaning and checking is being used.	0	1	2	3	4	
	15. The whole workplace is sparkling clean.	0	1	2	3	4	
Standardizing	16. There are standards for the elimination of unnecessary items.	0	1	2	3	4	
	17. Immediate action is taken if storage becomes disorderly.	0	1	2	3	4	/20
	18. Cleaning is initiated whenever if dirt is discovered.	0	1	2	3	4	
	19. The whole factory is clean inside and out.	0	1	2	3	4	
	20. The first three steps of 5S have become habitual.	0	1	2	3	4	
Training & Discipline	21. The boss is very active with regard to 5S.	0	1	2	3	4	
	22. All the workers are enthusiastic about 5S.	0	1	2	3	4	
	23. The boss gives stern criticism for disorder at the workplace.	0	1	2	3	4	/20
	24. Subordinates respond positively when criticized.	0	1	2	3	4	
	25. Everything is based on 4W1H.	0	1	2	3	4	
	Total marks						

128

Finally: Has 5S Become a Habit?

1. The factory where 5S has taken root

- So, what were the results of the "STEP II 5S Checklist"?
- If your total mark was below 30, it's a good idea to go back and review STEP I right away!

Checkpoint: Total marks

1. 0–30   **Unsatisfactory**   Back to STEP I!

2. 31–50   **Below Average**   Review STEP II, particularly those items with low scores, and redo the test

3. 51–70   **Average**   Needs reinforcement of weak points

4. 71–90   **Above Average**   But aim even higher

5. 91-100 **Excellent**   Keep up the good work!

2. Perfecting a 5S program in your factory

- 5S has gradually taken root and become habitual.
- The aim now is to join the ranks of the world's first-class companies in terms of 5S.
- And that means trying even harder!

Checkpoints

1. Clearing up *after* unnecessary items appear.
   → Clearing up so that unnecessary items don't appear.

2. Organizing *after* things become disordered
   → Organizing so that things never get disordered.

3. Cleaning *after* things get dirty
   → Cleaning so that things won't get dirty.

4. Standardizing to *avoid* mess
   → Standardizing so that mess becomes impossible.

5. *Compulsory* 5S
   → Spontaneous implementation of 5S.

Creating a 5S radar chart just as we did in STEP I

5S CHECKLIST (OFFICE)		Section	Checker				
		Marks /100	Previous marks /100	Date: / /			

5S	NO.	CHECKING ITEM	EVALUATION CRITERIA	MARKS				
				0	1	2	3	4
CLEARING UP (/20)	1	Lockers	No irrelevant reference materials, such as documents, drawings, meeting materials, etc.					
	2	Desks	No excess pieces of equipment or reference materials on desks or in drawers.					
	3	Visual control	Irrelevant items or documents can be identified at a glance.					
	4	Standards for disposal	Standards are fixed for disposal of documents and equipment.					
	5	Exhibits	Displays are up-to-date, tidy and well-balanced.					
ORGANIZING (/20)	6	Storage labels	Labeling of lockers and equipment allows immediate identification.					
	7	Labels for documents and equipment	Everything is clearly identified.					
	8	Ease of use	Storage is designed for ease of use.					
	9	Orderly storage	Everything is stored in a fixed place.					
	10	Aisles and display areas	All dividing lines and bulletin boards are clearly indicated.					
CLEANING (/20)	11	Floor	The floor is clean.					
	12	Dust and dirt	Windows, windowsills and shelves are clean.					
	13	Cleaning responsibilities	There is a rotation or shift system for cleaning.					
	14	Wastebaskets	There is a system for getting rid of dirt and waste paper.					
	15	Habitual cleaning	Sweeping and dusting are regarded as habitual activities.					

STEP · II

5S	NO.	CHECKING ITEM	EVALUATION CRITERIA	MARKS				
				0	1	2	3	4
STANDARDIZING (/20)	16	Ventilation	The air is clean, odorless and free of cigarette smoke.					
	17	Lighting	The angle and intensity of illumination are appropriate.					
	18	Uniforms	Nobody is wearing a dirty uniform.					
	19	Environment	The general environment is good, including color, air, lighting, etc.					
	20	The first 3 Steps	There is a system for maintaining Clearing Up, Organizing and Cleaning.					
TRAINING & DISCIPLINE (/20)	21	Clothing rules	The rules are adhered to.					
	22	Interaction of people	There is a pleasant general atmosphere, people exchange greetings, etc.					
	23	Meeting times and break times	Everyone makes an effort to be punctual.					
	24	Telephone manners	Everyone states their business clearly, politely and succinctly.					
	25	Rules and regulations	All rules and regulations are strictly observed.					
Total		Check dispersal of marks (total for each column)						

5S CHECKLIST (PRODUCTION DEPT.)		Section	Checker				
		Marks /100	Previous marks /100	Date: / /			

5S	NO.	CHECKING ITEM	EVALUATION CRITERIA	MARKS				
				0	1	2	3	4
CLEARING UP (/20)	1	Parts or materials	No unnecessary stock items or work-in-progress.					
	2	Machines and equipment	All machines and pieces of equipment are in regular use.					
	3	Jigs, tools and molds	All jigs, tools, molds, cutting tools and fittings are in regular use.					
	4	Visual control	All unnecessary items can be distinguished at a glance.					
	5	Standards for disposal	There are clear standards for eliminating excess.					
ORGANIZING (/20)	6	Storage labels	There are labels to indicate different *districts* and *sub-districts*.					
	7	Labels shelves and stored items	All shelves and items in storage are labeled clearly.					
	8	Quantity indicators	There are clear indications of maximum and miminum stock quantities.					
	9	Dividing lines	Dividing lines are all clear and all painted white.					
	10	Jigs and tools	Storage of jigs and tools is well organized for ease of extraction and return.					
CLEANING (/20)	11	Floor	The floor is always clean and shining.					
	12	Machines	Machines are kept clean.					
	13	Cleaning and checking	Cleaning and checking are regarded as the same thing.					
	14	Cleaning responsibilities	There is a rotation or shift system for cleaning.					
	15	Habitual cleaning	Sweeping and wiping are regarded as habitual activities.					

5S	NO.	CHECKING ITEM	EVALUATION CRITERIA	MARKS				
				0	1	2	3	4
STANDARDIZING (/20)	16	Ventilation	The air is clean and odorless.					
	17	Lighting	The angle and intensity of illumination are appropriate.					
	18	Work clothes	Nobody is wearing dirty or oil-stained work clothes.					
	19	Avoidance of dirt	Emphasis is placed on avoiding the accumulation of dirt.					
	20	The first 3 Steps	There is a system for maintaining Clearing Up, Organizing and Cleaning.					
TRAINING & DISCIPLINE (/20)	21	Clothing rules	The rules are adhered to.					
	22	Interaction of people	There is a pleasant general atmosphere, people exchange greetings, etc.					
	23	Meeting and smoking	Everyone strives to be punctual and observe smoking regulations.					
	24	Rules and procedures	All rules and work procedures are acknowledged and respected.					
	25	Observation of rules	All rules and regulations are strictly observed.					
Total		Check dispersal of marks (total for each column)						

134

STEP II
5S Radar Chart

Section	
Date	

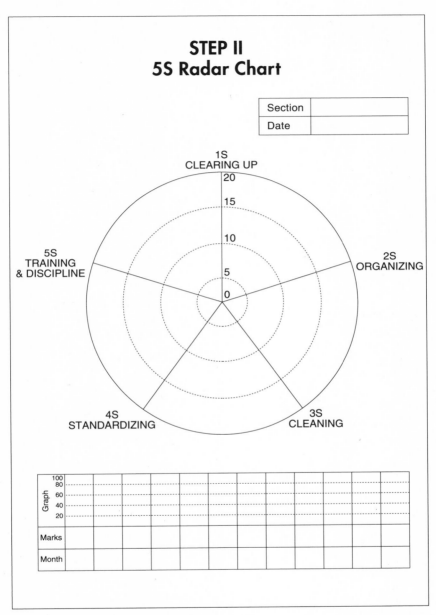

© JIT Management Laboratory Co., Ltd.

STEP

III

TAKING 5S TO A HIGHER LEVEL
(Preventive 5S)

PREPARATION:
Evaluating the Factory
Where 5S Has Become Habitual

■ Before taking 5S to a higher level in STEP III, let's evaluate the present situation using the "STEP II 5S Checklist."

Checkpoints

 1. With less than 50 marks, you cannot proceed on to STEP III.

2. Between 51 and 90 marks, you must review all the weak points in your factory.

3. If your total is over 91 marks, you can move straight on to STEP III.

STEP II Radar Chart

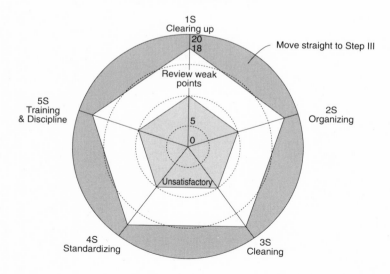

PROCESS 1:
AVOIDING UNNECESSARY ITEMS
(*PREVENTIVE* CLEARING UP)

1-1. Why Do Unnecessary Items Still Appear?

- If you have any excess items, they must be sorted out using red tags.
- But if that kind of clearing up has become habitual, why are there *still* unnecessary items?

Checkpoints

1. Making clearing up habitual is a fundamental process.

2. If there are any unnecessary items, you must ask WHY?

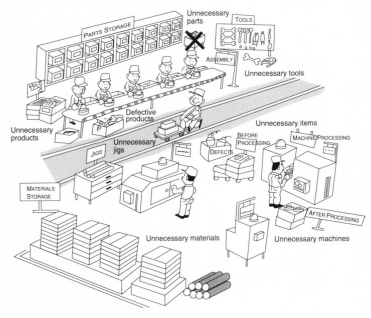

1-2. Changing Attitudes Toward Clearing Up
— from *Remedial* Clearing Up to
Preventive Clearing Up

■ Clearing up after unnecessary items appear is important, but it's preferable to ensure that they do not appear at all.

Checkpoints

Instead of doing *Remedial* Clearing Up every time unnecessary items appear, is it possible to implement *Preventive* Clearing Up, which means clearing up so that no unnecessary items will appear?

 1. Switch from "Unnecessary items appear → Clear up" to "Unnecessary items appear → Why?"

2. After asking 5 WHYs, consider HOW to remedy the situation:

WHY 1:
"Why do unnecessary items appear?"

↓

They come from the previous process.

↓

WHY 2:
"Why do they come from the previous process?"

↓

Because the previous process produces them.

↓

WHY 3:
"Why does the previous process produce them?"

↓

Because that was the order from the management.

↓

WHY 4:
"Why did the management give that order?"

↓

Because changes in plans were too late.

↓

WHY 5:
"Why were the changes in plans too late?"

↓

Because manufacturing throughput time is too long.

↓

Change to one-part-at-a-time production.

↓

Why do unnecessary items appear?

1-3. Creating a System with No Waste and No Excess

1. Rationalizing the system

> ■ Rationalize your system so that you don't produce excess, and you won't have to worry about getting rid of it!
> ■ This is called *"Preventive Clearing Up."*

Checkpoints

1. Repeat WHY? five times.

2. Use NIED (New IE Method).

3. The basis is 4W1H.

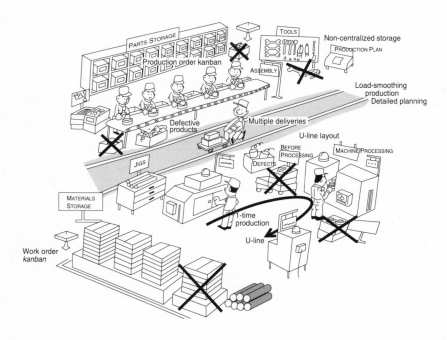

2. Leveled production

- A production schedule which only produces a certain item once or twice a month in bulk is called *lot production*.
- The tendency with this method is to accumulate unnecessary items in the processing and assembly departments and the products storage warehouse.
- That's why leveled production is recommended. It is also known as load-smoothing production.

Checkpoints

 1. Calculate the Cycle Time for each product.

$$\frac{\text{Monthly production}}{\text{Work days}} = \text{Daily production} \implies \frac{\text{Work hours per day}}{\text{Daily production}} = \text{Cycle Time}$$

2. Create a production schedule by allocating products according to the cycle time.

3. If you cannot create exclusive lines, use mixed flow production.

4. Parts supply and line balance are the main themes of mixed flow production.

Lot Production
Monthly

	Early	Mid	Late	
A	20			20
B		20		20
C			20	20

⬇

Leveled Production
Monthly

	Early	Mid	Late	
A	I piece per day		20	
B	I piece per day		20	
C	I piece per day		20	

For printed circuit boards, try mixed flow assembly

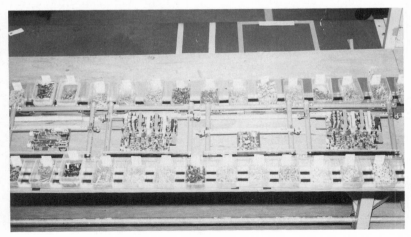

3. Production order *kanban*

■ Do you sometimes have unnecessary items in the materials warehouses and the warehouse for standard and customized parts?

■ It's the result of ordering too many items just in case they might be needed some day.

■ Work order *kanban* are used to place small orders for items that are definitely needed in the next process.

Checkpoints

1. The *3 Keys* are essential for parts and materials.

2. In particular, fix maximum and minimum quantities.

3. Put *kanban* on parts and materials.

4. If *kanban* are removed, order only for the amount indicated.

Make full use of a kanban despatch board

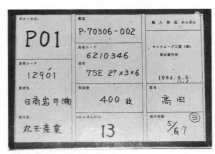

Kanban

Despatch board

4. Multiple deliveries

- In order to get rid of unnecessary items, dealing with requests in detail is the main point.
- The same can be said for deliveries into the factory.
- Lot deliveries of large quantities at the same time on a regular basis, for example once a month, tend to pile up unnecessary items.
- This should be replaced by multiple small-lot deliveries as needed.

Checkpoints

1. The 3 Keys are essential for storage for delivered items.

2. Maximum stock quantity should be marked in red.

3. Reduce the maximum quantity level.

4. By controlling the quantity, increase the number of deliveries.

Reduced quantities improve the production flow

5. Creating lines

- Traditional job-shop type layout, with the same machines grouped together, tends to lead to batch production.
- With batch production you cannot avoid unnecessary items.

Checkpoints

1. **Awareness revolution**
   Get rid of your old ways of thinking

2. **Job-shop elimination**
   Do away with group layout of identical machines

3. **Process flow diagram**
   List machines in order of use according to each product

4. **Line creation**
   Create a new layout of machines according to the process flow

A U-Line is a fine example of production flow-oriented layout

6. Work order *kanban*

- Is a separate work schedule used for each process?
- This results in uneven production.
- Each product is produced in relation to many processes.

Checkpoints

1. "A lathe is lathe, a press is a press." Stop using separate work schedules for each process.

2. Do assembly according to a leveled production schedule.

3. Attach *kanban* including production instructions to the parts required for assembly — *Work order kanban*

4. Implement processing of only the number of items indicated on the *kanban*.

Work Order Kanban	
Storage 02-025-4002	**Post No.** P01
Name of Item F.	**No. of Item** 20010589
Quality SV53/6	**Quantity** 20
	Post No. P01
	Plating Control No. 20010589
	Responsible person

148

The basic rule is to produce in the order that *kanban* are removed

7. One-piece-at-a-time manufacturing

- Are you doing large lot production because you don't like changing the type of machines or you think changing the setup is a lot of trouble?
- The result is the production of a large number of items unnecessary at that particular time.

Checkpoints

 1. Level out production planning.

2. Don't produce anything which is not required by the leveled production plan.

3. Create a line layout.

4. Stop lot production and finish products one by one
   — One-piece-at-a-time manufacturing.

5. At all stages during processing, one-touch setup is important.

One-by-one is the one and only way

8. Flexible planning

- How many times a month do you produce a production plan?
- And how often do you have to revise it?
- The worst thing is to produce a production plan only once a month for presentation to the shopfloor.
- What is needed is more flexible planning.

Checkpoints

1. Check in detail the stocks of products.

2. The production plan should reflect present product stock levels.

3. Revise the production plan in a more detailed way.

4. Inform the workplace of detailed changes to the plan.

Inflexible Planning

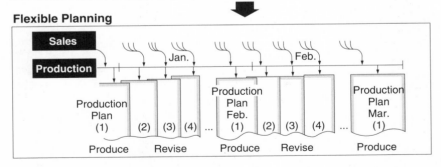

151

PROCESS 2:
AVOIDING DISORGANIZATION
(*PREVENTIVE* Organizing)

2-1. Why Is There Still Disorganization?

> ■ You can return jigs and tools to their original places and try to organize properly, but things still get in a mess.
> ■ Have you ever thought WHY this happens?

Checkpoints

 1. Organizing consists of three points: finding the items, getting at them, and returning them.

2. Returning and organizing *should* be a habit.

3. So why is there still a problem?

"Why is there still a mess?"

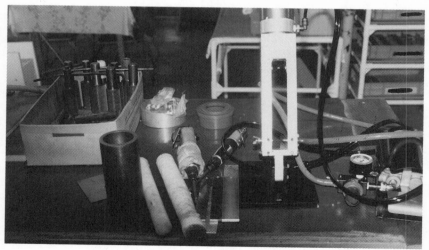

2-2. Changing Attitudes Toward Organizing — from *Remedial* Organizing to *Preventive* Organizing

- You return all jigs and tools to the proper places and maintain proper organization.
- You keep all inventory in the proper place. You make a habit of doing this.
- But isn't there some better way to avoid problems altogether?

Checkpoints

Instead of *Remedial* Organizing every time jigs and tools get disorganized, is it possible to implement *Preventive* Organizing, which means organizing so that they *never* get in a mess?

 1. Switch your way of thinking from "things are disorganized, so we must fix them up" to "things are disorganized, why are they like that?"

2. Then ask 5 WHYs, and consider HOW you can do something about it.

2-3. *Preventive* Organizing for Storage Places

1. Why does storage get in disarray?

- Now, more specifically, why does storage for materials, parts and products get in a mess?
- There are various possible reasons.
- Let's investigate them.

Checkpoints

 1. If you find disorder in the storage, apply five WHYs? and one HOW? to discover the real reason.

2. You'll probably discover that the reasons for disorder are these:

- The storage place is not fixed at all or it's not fixed very clearly.
  → Apply 5S thoroughly, especially the *3 Keys*.

- The rules and regulations are not adhered to.
  → Increased discipline throughout the company and move from"making rules" to "making systems."

- More items are stocked than were originally allowed for by the *3 Keys*.
  → Create a system which includes only necessary items (*kanban*).

"Why did it get like this?"

2. A system where things have to be stored in a specific place

- The main reason for disorder is that 5S is not being implemented properly.
- As you would expect, factories which do not strictly apply the 3 Keys get very messy.

Checkpoints

 1. The 3 Keys of fixing position, items, and quantity must be strictly applied to storage shelves.

2. The 3 Keys must be strictly applied by those responsible for replacing and extracting items stored on shelves.

3. For storage of work-in-progress there are 4 basic points:
   - lines to mark storage area
   - name of storage area
   - indication of previous and next processes
   - indication of quantity

4. The 3 Keys must be strictly applied by those responsible for replacing and extracting work-in-progress.

5. Along with the discipline to organize and store items, it's necessary to create a system in which each item has its own unique *address*.

"Everything has to be systematized!"

3. Discipline is crucial to maintaining a well-ordered workplace

- Humans are the core factor in all production.
- In particular, how the staff thinks has a strong influence on the quality of production.
- That's why general company discipline is very important.

Checkpoints

 1. Section chiefs, department managers, and factory managers should all make regular shopfloor inspections:

- Section chiefs .... at least twice every morning and three times during the afternoon.
- Department managers ...... at least once every morning and twice every afternoon.
- Factory managers .... at least once every morning and once every afternoon.

2. It's important that people should not only be able to give constructive criticism but also to accept it.

3. Team spirit and commitment are the bases for all factory behavior.

4. Rules, regulations and standards should be clearly displayed, noticed and acted upon.

"Make this one step lower!"

4. Is that part really required?

- All too often, items above and beyond the limits fixed by the *3 Keys* are delivered or sent on from the previous process.
- As a result, the storage place naturally gets overcrowded.
- But WHY do these things get sent on?

Checkpoints

 1. The *3 Keys* should be applied to all storage, with particular emphasis on maximum and minimum quantity levels.

2. Even if there are more items than are stipulated by the maximum quantity level, that doesn't mean you should change the level to match the items.

3. Investigate the real reasons why there are too many items.

4. Here are the major reasons and suggested countermeasures:
   - Infrequent deliveries   → Multiple deliveries
   - Bulk supply of parts   → Small lot supply
   - Over-production   → Production to meet orders
   - Large lots   → Small lot production
   - Just-in-case ordering   → Ordering only the required number

   - Push production initiated by previous process → Pull production initiated by next process (*kanban*)
   - Long changeover time   → One-touch setup
   - Lot production   → Leveled production

5. In order to clarify the needs above, keep quantities as low as possible.

"What are those empty crates doing there?"

2-4. *Preventive* Organizing for Jigs and Tools

1. Why do jigs and tools get disorganized?

- Why do jigs and tools get in a mess?
- This mostly happens when they are returned after use.
- But is there any way to avoid having to return them?

Checkpoints

1. Three points about jigs and tools:
   - Identifying .... All jigs and tools are clear at a glance.
   - Taking out .... Easier extraction for easier use.
   - Returning .... Easy to return after use.

2. What's the basic difference between materials and parts and jigs and tools?
   - Materials and parts .... After attachment to products, they never return.
   - Jigs and tools .... After use, they are put away.

3. Most disorder occurs during the returning process.

"Why do we have to return them?"

162

2. Ideas for easier return

■ If the main reason for disorder is the process of returning items to their proper place, what is needed is a way to make the process easier.

Checkpoints

1. Storage places shaped to fit the items — Organizing by shape

2. Return to the appropriate color — Organizing by color

3. Abandon centralized storage — Storage at each machine

4. Abandon storage by type — Storage by procedure

5. Ensure fumble-free storage — Enlarge dimensions of storage devices

6. Eliminated the need to stretch — Storage close to point of use (tools within 10cms of your hand)

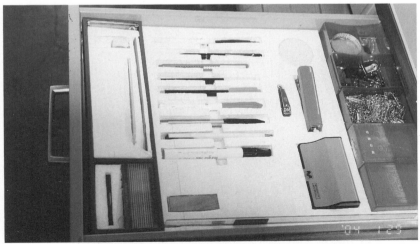

Organizing by shape for office items

3. Eliminating the need to return

- You've thought up various ideas to improve the process of returning items.
- But if this doesn't eliminate all problems, then what is needed is more training to develop ideas for doing away with the need to return items.

Checkpoints

 1. Try suspending the tools, so that after use, you simply let them go...automatic organization.

2. After use, you "return" the item, but as a result the storage gets disorganized, so find a way to avoid the need to return....

3. You can often see this in action at a dentist's office or in bars with hoses for dispensing soft drinks.

4. Hang the items at point of use, within your reach.

5. If hanging tools get in the way, use magnets or guide-wires to keep them from swinging free.

Automatic organization

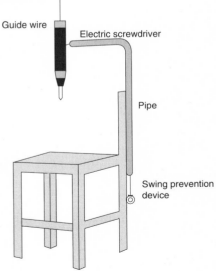

Guide wire

Electric screwdriver

Pipe

Swing prevention device

4. Cutting down the number of jigs and tools

- Now there is less need to return jigs and tools.
- However, the jigs and tools still have to be used.
- But let's face it, the fewer jigs and tools you use, the fewer problems you'll have!

Checkpoints

You should ask simple questions like "Are all these tools really necessary?" → Consider reducing the number of jigs and tools.

1. Could one tool do the work or two?

2. In order to do that, greater standardization of parts may be necessary to reduce the number of tools.

Reduction in number of tools

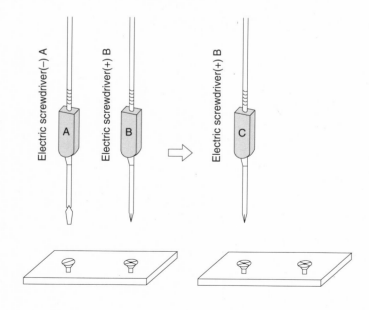

5. Getting rid of jigs and tools altogether

- By consolidating, you can greatly reduce the number of jigs and tools you need to use.
- But if you could get rid of them altogether, it would make life much easier!

Checkpoints

Ask the question "Why do we need to use these tools in the first place?"

1. Are there any possible alternatives?

2. Ask yourself what you would need if there weren't any jigs and tools.

Alternatives to jigs and tools

"How do we get rid of this crescent wrench?"

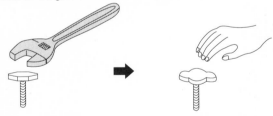

"Why do we need to use this allen wrench?"

6. Alternative ways of doing the work

■ We've now thought of some ways to get rid of jigs and tools. But now let's think at a slightly deeper level about simplifying the production process.

Checkpoints

This time you should think about the actual methods being used rather than the tools: e.g."Why do we have to use screws?"

 1. What is the essential purpose of this operation in the production process (e.g. inserting screws)?

2. Is there some alternative method to achieve the same result?

3. Will the quality be satisfactory with another method? What is the cheapest method?

Ask questions about everything in the factory!
Rather than looking for problems in the way you do things now, ask why you are doing them like that in the first place.

"Why are we using screws?"   But wouldn't glue do just as well?
To put things together (purpose)

PROCESS 3:
CLEANING WITHOUT GETTING DIRTY AGAIN
(*PREVENTIVE* CLEANING)

3-1. Why Does it Get Dirty?

- Whenever the floor or the machines get dirty, immediate cleaning has by now become a habitual response.
- But that is no reason for getting complacent!
- "Why does the floor get dirty again?" This is what you have to consider carefully.

Checkpoints

1. Cleaning starts with picking up a broom or grabbing a duster.

2. Make it a habit to take immediate action as soon as something gets dirty.

3. Ask yourself "Where does the dirt on the floor and the dust and oil on the machines come from?"

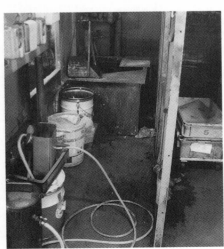

**The factory manager's complaint:
"It's impossible to keep things clean!"**

3-2. Changing Attitudes about Cleaning

■ It's important to clean up as soon as something gets dirty, but how do you prevent dirt from reappearing?

Checkpoints

Instead of doing Remedial Cleaning every time the floor, walls, machines or equipment get dirty, is it possible to institute Preventive Cleaning, so that they never get dirty again?

 1. Switch from "Floors and machines get dirty, so clean them up" to "Floors and machines get dirty, but WHY?"

2. Unless the causes of dirt are eliminated, dirt will surely reappear. Point: "Eliminate the cause, eliminate the problem!"

What could be the cause of the dirt here?

3-3. Dirt Gets Everywhere

■ Dirt can easily take over if you don't do anything about it, just like pollution in the air or the sea.
■ The first priority is to stop this tendency.

Checkpoints

1. Dirt in the factory includes: dust, dirt, trash, soot, chips, leftover materials, oil, dirty water, etc.

2. Factors involved in the spread of dirt throughout the factory: wind, water, oil, workers' uniforms, the soles of shoes, tires (e.g. forklifts).

3. If you wait until the dirts spread around, you'll have to expend more energy to do the cleaning!

Dirt spreads around before anyone realizes it

Chips

Spreading around on footwear

Spread around on tires

3-4. Sources of Dirt and Grime

1. Getting at the source

- Dust on the windowsill doesn't emerge from inside the sill itself!
- Chips on the floor don't come out of the floor!
- In the majority of cases, dirt comes from somewhere else.
- And the dirt brings with it the trouble of having to clean!

Checkpoints

1. Look for any dirt, evidence of dirt and grime.

2. If you find any dirt, think where it could have come from.

3. As first did, prevent further spread.

4. Then look for the source.

5. Then deal with grime at the source.

6. Finally think about methods to prevent the grime being produced in the first place: e.g. chipless drilling.

"Which countermeasure is more effective?"

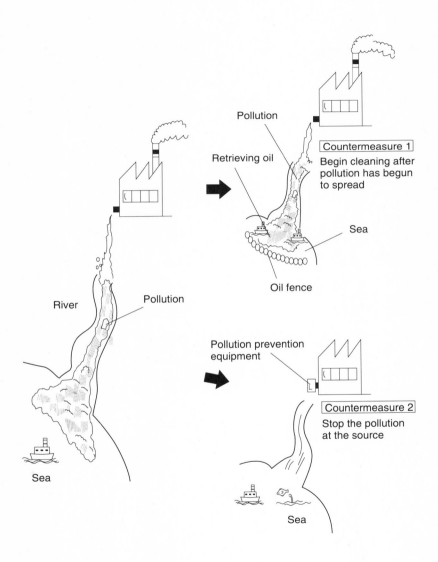

Pollution

Retrieving oil

Countermeasure 1
Begin cleaning after
pollution has begun
to spread

Sea

Oil fence

River   Pollution

Pollution prevention
equipment

Countermeasure 2
Stop the pollution
at the source

Sea

Sea

STEP · III

173

2. Where do chips on the floor come from?

- You often see chips and filings scattered around on the floors near machining processes.
- They are not only dangerous, they can also affect the accuracy of processing.
- Where do they come from?

Checkpoints

 1. Do thorough cleaning. The floor is the best indication of problems in the factory, so polish it until it shines!

2. After polishing, be on the lookout for the reappearance of dirt and grime.

3. Then immediately ask "Where does that dirt come from?" "Why does it occur?"

4. As a first countermeasure, screen off the machine with cardboard.

5. If the floor still gets dirty, enlarge the cardboard screen.

6. Finally, aim for a machine which produces zero chips.

Creating a chip-free machine

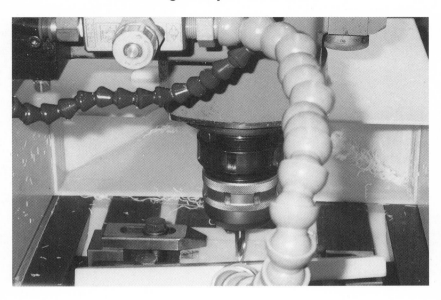

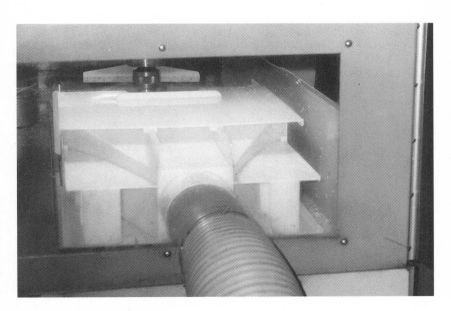

3. Where does oil on the floor come from?

- The floors around cutting machines and presses are often sticky.
- The reason is, of course, oil.
- Oil from the machines leaks out and spreads around, making the floor sticky for a long period.
- You should aim to have a floor on which you could safely walk in white socks!

Checkpoints

1. You should get rid of the idea that "You can't avoid grime when you work with oil!"

2. First, completely remove all the oil accumulated on the floor and then implement thorough cleaning using detergents.

3. Remove all oil fences and oil-pans.

4. Once the fences and pans have been removed, the oil will flow on to the polished floor.

5. Now you can see exactly where the oil is coming from and determine how to stop it.

"Ah, it's not surprising the floor gets tacky!"

4. Where does sand on the floor come from?

- The floor of casting plants tend to look like deserts, because they're covered with sand.
- But where does the sand come from?

Checkpoints

1. Stop thinking of the sand on the floor as the way things have got to be.

2. Sand falls from worktables where cores are finished.

3. Create a gutter around the table for the sand to collect in.

4. Construct a shield around the table to prevent spattering.

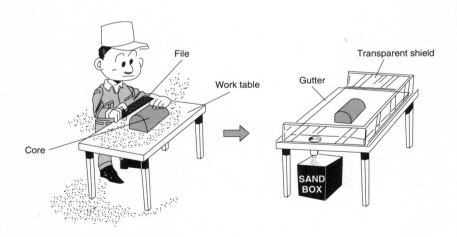

File

Work table

Core

Gutter

Transparent shield

SAND BOX

5. Systems to prevent dust and dirt getting in from the outside

■ Up to now, we've concentrated on eliminating the chips, oil and dust that come from machines.
■ But some of the grime inside the factory comes from outside, and this should also be eliminated.

Checkpoints

 1. Completely clean all factory floors and machines.

2. Ask questions like, "Where did this dirt come from?" "How did this dust get there?"

3. The dirt and grime that can't be accounted for by sources inside the factory must have come from the outside.

4. Find the sources.

5. Create countermeasures to prevent dirt coming through windows, etc.
   — Double shields and vinyl curtains could be the solution.

6. Remember that people and vehicles (such as forklifts) can also bring in dirt from outside.

Mop

Mop

Mops attached to carts and forklifts

PROCESS 4:
PREVENTING DEGRADATION OF THE ENVIRONMENT
(*PREVENTIVE* STANDARDIZING)

4-1. Tidiness Reflects Efficiency

■ When you go on a trip, you sometimes feel impressed by the cleanliness and neatness of a place.
■ It may be because there is no rubbish lying around, there are tidy, tree-lined avenues, or the houses are all painted in pleasant colors...other words, it strikes you as being a pleasant, well-ordered environment in which to live or work.

Checkpoints

1. Tidiness and cleanliness reflect overall efficiency.

2. In the factory:

   a. There are NO unnecessary items
   b. There is NO disorder 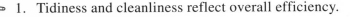 3 NOs
   c. There is NO dirt in the workplace

   These three NOs + the discipline to maintain them
   = TIDINESS

3. The secret of *Preventive Standardizing* lies in full application of Preventive 3S (Preventive Clearing Up, Preventive Organizing and Preventive Cleaning).

Preventive Standardizing

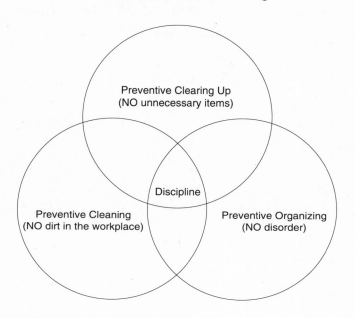

Preventive Clearing Up
(NO unnecessary items)

Discipline

Preventive Cleaning
(NO dirt in the workplace)

Preventive Organizing
(NO disorder)

4-2. Preventing Excess

■ How many different systems do you have in your factory to prevent the emergence of unnecessary items?

Checkpoint

When inspecting the factory, it's important to understand the present situation accurately by applying the following *Preventive Clearing Up Checklist*.

If the total is below 7 marks, it's necessary to start STEP III again.

No	Check Item	Content	Marks		/10
			0	1	2
1	Awareness	What do you think about unnecessary items?	Nothing can be done about them	Want to do something	Trying hard to eliminate them
2	Leveled Production	How often do you make a production plan?	Once a month	4 times a month	Daily
3	Kanban	Do you use work order kanban and order kanban?	Use neither	Use them partly	Widely used
4	Production Flow	Have you created lines or use one-piece-at-a-time production?	Hardly at all	Many lines created and working toward one-piece-at-a-time production	One-piece-at-a-time production widely used
5	Delivery	How often are parts purchased and made-to-order parts delivered?	Once a month	Once a week	Daily

Preventive Clearing Up Checklist

181

4-3. Preventing Disorganization

> ■ Have you managed to properly organize all storage areas?

Checkpoint

"A disorganized workplace is the sign of disorganized thinking."

Even if you sometimes get disorganized yourself because you are so busy, it's important to maintain order in the workplace by implementing Preventive Organizing.

Let's check the situation using the following checklist.

If the total is below 7 marks, it's necessary to start STEP III again.

Preventive Organizing Checklist

No	Check Item	Content	Marks		/10
			0	1	2
1	Awareness	What do you think about storage?	Nothing can be done about it	Want to do something	Trying hard to avoid it
2	5S • 3 Keys	Are the basic storage principles applied to the shopfloor and work sites?	Hardly applied	Applied to a large extent	Almost completely applied
3	Rules for Storage Areas	Are rules kept when items are brought in or taken out?	Hardly at all	Partly kept	Mostly kept
4	Systems for Storage Areas	Are FIFO and *suspending* in use?	Hardly at all	Partly used	Used in most cases
5	Jigs and Tools	Are systems in place to avoid the need to return items or avoid their use altogether?	Hardly at all	Partly in use	Used in most cases

182

4-4. Preventing Grime

> ■ How many different systems do you have in the factory to prevent the spread of dirt or its occurence in the first place?

Checkpoint

Next we need to check what measures are taken to prevent grime. To what extent is Preventive Cleaning in use?

Let's check using the following checklist.

If the total is below 7 marks, it's necessary to start STEP III again.

x

Preventive Cleaning Checklist

No	Check Item	Content	Marks /10 0	1	2
1	Awareness	What do you think about dirt in the workplace?	Nothing can be done about it	Want to do something	Trying hard to get rid of it
2	Floors	Is the floor shining?	It's covered with dirt, dust, chips & oil	It's fairly clean	It's clean enough to walk around in white socks
3	Walls • Windows • Toilets	Are they dirty and dusty?	Covered with dust and dirt	Cleaning is done every day	A system is also in use to prevent dirt and dust getting in
4	Machines	Are they grimy and sticky?	They're very grimy and sticky	Daily cleaning is done	Cleaning and checking is done thoroughly
5	System to prevent the emergence of dirt	To what extent are systems in use to avoid dirt?	Hardly at all	Fairly well developed	There is a system in use everywhere

STEP · III

183

4-5. Maintaining Standardization and Tidiness

- By grasping all the points about Preventive 3S and also by increasing standardization, you are on the way to becoming a showcase 5S factory.

Checkpoint

You need to understand all the weak points of your factory, focus on efforts to improve them, and develop all your strengths.

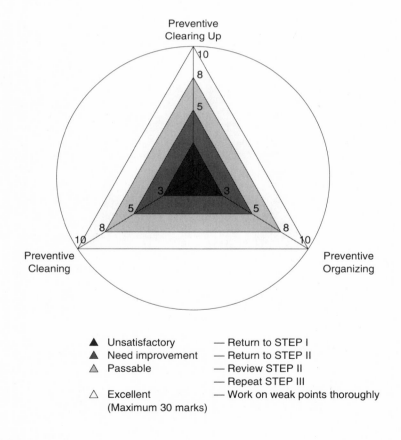

▲ Unsatisfactory	— Return to STEP I
▲ Need improvement	— Return to STEP II
△ Passable	— Review STEP II
	— Repeat STEP III
△ Excellent	— Work on weak points thoroughly
(Maximum 30 marks)	

184

PROCESS 5:
SYSTEMATIZING TRAINING
(*PREVENTIVE* TRAINING & DISCIPLINE)

5-1. Rules Rather Than Criticism, Systems Rather Than Rules

- We've already seen that it is important to be good at giving constructive criticism.
- But is this criticism developed into rules?

Checkpoints

1. Do managers and supervisors regularly inspect the workplace?

2. Using 4W1H, is everyone good at giving and receiving criticism.

3. Rules made to cover all the points that prompted criticism.

4. But simply having rules is not enough because everyone has to keep them in mind.

5. Create a system whereby the work will automatically be done in the proper way.

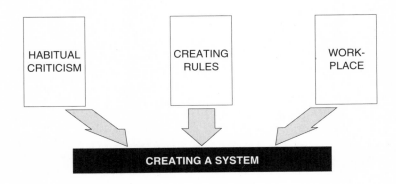

185

5-2. Defects Caused by Careless Mistakes
→ Constructive Criticism
→ Mistake-Proofing

- When mistakes are caused by carelessness, constructive criticism is, of course, necessary.
- But it is a fact that everyone makes mistakes sometimes.
- Isn't there some system that can avoid defects even when mistakes are made?

Checkpoints

 1. Humans make mistakes.
But the number of mistakes can be reduced
→ Education • Discipline

2. Create a system which does not lead to defects even when there are mistakes
→ Mistake-proofing

3. Mistake-proofing means the prevention of defects by eliminating defects at the source.

[Processing mistakes] Preventing drilling defects

Problem Point: When using a drill press, the operator sometimes returned before completely drilling the hole. The improperly drilled holes caused problems during assembly.

Before improvement:

The drill was supposed to go down completely while drilling, but it was sometimes returning too early, creating defects. Whether the holes were properly drilled or not was left up to the judgment of the operators. Most defects only became apparent during the assembly process.

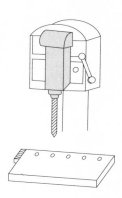

After improvement:

Two limit switches were attached (L/S). If L/S1 is released before L/S2 has been activated, a buzzer sounds to inform operators of a drilling defect.

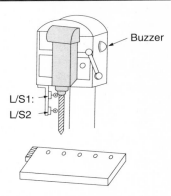

Buzzer

L/S1:
L/S2

L/S1: Switch to confirm
start of drilling
L/S2 Switch to confirm proper
drill insertion

5-3. Careless Mistakes with Safety
→ Constructive Criticism → Rules
→ Safety *Mistake-Proofing*

> - A little carelessness can easily lead to an accident.
> - But constructive criticism is not much use once an accident has occurred.
> - What we want to do is create a workplace where safety is the main focus.

Checkpoints

 1. Safety is everyone's main priority.

2. The important thing is to systematize safety mistake-proofing rather than just reprimand people for not sticking to the rules.

[Safety with cranes] Preventing accidents from rough operation
Problem point: The crane was saddle hitting a stopper. As a result, items being carried sometimes fell off the hook.

Before improvement:

There was a stopper attached to the rail limiting the movement of the crane saddle. If the crane moved too fast, the saddle sometimes crashed into the stopper, causing the items being carried to shake violently or even fall off the hook.

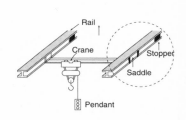

After improvement:

When the limit switch attached to the saddle touches the metal fitting, the crane stops before hitting the stopper. No accidents have occured since the improvement was made.

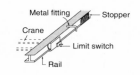

188

5-4. Making Training & Discipline a Habit

1. 5S Months

- Training and discipline is basically a question of people's attitudes.
- But it's difficult to do much on your own.
- What's needed to anchor training and discipline is the commitment and involvement of the whole company.

Checkpoints

1. Several months should be selected during the year as periods for the whole company to implement 5S.

2. These are known as *5S Months*, and there should be at least two every year.

3. Banners and other displays should be used prominently during a 5S Month.

4. Various events should be held, including 5S seminars and 5S contests.

STEP · III

"Futhering 5S Activities" (Japan)

"5S in Mind and Body: Awareness for the Head, Clearing Up and Organizing for the Hands" (South Korea)

"Eliminating Waste Through 5S" (South Korea)

2. 5S Patrols

- Ideally, once a month the factory manager and other top executives should make a tour of inspection around the factory concentrating on 5S.
- They should evaluate each section in terms of 5S progress.

Checkpoints

1. Fix a regular date for the 5S patrol (e.g. the third Friday every month).

2. The patrol should include top management, such as the company president and the factory manager.

3. There should be a fixed inspection route.

4. 5S evaluation marks should be given to each section.

5. The patrol should listen to the comments and opinions of workplace operators, and offer advice as appropriate.

"Hmm. Things are looking better!" — President

3. 5S Contests

> ■ It's a good idea to hold 5S contests several times a year, or, if possible, once a month.

Checkpoints

1. Implement regular 5S patrols.
2. 5S evaluation marks should be given to each section.
3. Hold a 5S contest involving all the operators in the workplace.
4. 5S badges can be awarded to the best workplaces and the winner can be given some kind of prize.

5S badges and a 5S ribbon

5S display

4. A 5S Newsletter

- Another effective idea is to start a 5S newsletter.
- It's not always easy to give sufficient education at the workplace.
- 5-minute 5S lessons can be held at morning or evening meetings based on points in the 5S newsletter.

Checkpoints

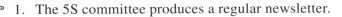

1. The 5S committee produces a regular newsletter.

2. It's published once or twice every month.

3. On publication date, it's handed out to line staff by section chiefs.

4. 5-minute 5S lessons can be held at morning or evening meetings based on points in the newsletter.

5. Effective contents include interesting ideas about 5S, with examples from both the technical and administrative sides, and comments from individual workers. Illustrations are also particularly helpful.

STEP · III

FINALLY:
Has Your Factory Become
A First-Class 5S Factory?

- It's time to fill in the 5S Checklist and the 5S Radar Chart.
- Did you get a perfect score?

5S Radar Chart

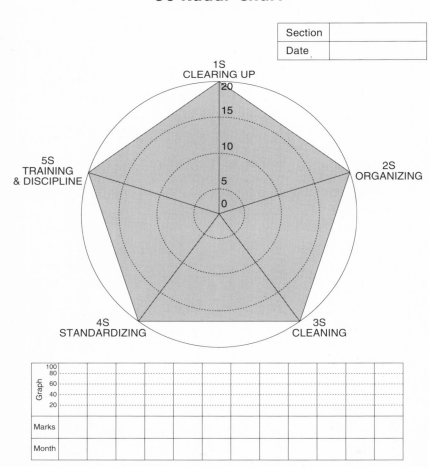

Index

About the Author

HIROYUKI HIRANO was born in Tokyo in 1946. After graduating from the department of industrial administration of Senshu University in 1970, he worked for the consulting division of a large software development company. He produced the first total production management system in Japan. Later he founded JIT Management Laboratory. Convinced that JIT is a powerful technique for thoroughly eliminating waste, he has been active in helping not only Japanese companies but also companies overseas mainly in South Korea, France and U.S.A. to streamline production, sales and distribution with JIT approach. His books include *JIT Implementation Manual: The Complete Guide to Just-In-Time Manufacturing* (Productivity Press, 1990) and *POKA-YOKE: Mistake-Proofing for Zero Defects* (PHP Institute, Inc., 1994).